HEROES OF THE REFORMATION

LIFE-CHANGING LESSONS FOR THE YOUNG

HEROES

OF THE REFORMATION

BY THE

REV. RICHARD NEWTON, D.D.

AUTHOR OF

The Life of Jesus Christ for the Young,
The King's Highway: The Ten Commandments for the Young

Solid Ground Christian Books
Birmingham, Alabama USA

Solid Ground Christian Books
2090 Columbiana Rd, Suite 2000
Birmingham, AL 35216
205-443-0311
sgcb@charter.net
http://solid-ground-books.com

Heroes of the Reformation
LIFE-CHANGING LESSONS FOR THE YOUNG

Richard Newton (1813-1887)

Taken from 1885 edition by The American Sunday School Union

Solid Ground Classic Reprints

First printing of new edition June 2005

Cover work by Borgo Design, Tuscaloosa, AL
Contact them at nelbrown@comcast.net

Cover painting is entitled "Sale of Tyndale's Bibles" and is found on page 115 of this volume.

ISBN: 1-932474-83-8

PREFACE.

In his epistle to the early Christians the apostle James exhorts them to "Take the prophets for an example." It is clear from this that God intended the characters of the good men, whose lives are written in his word, should be carefully studied by his people in after ages for their own profit and improvement. And if this is the right use to make of the histories of the "holy men of old," of whom we read in the Bible, then it is proper for us to make a similar use of the examples of God's faithful servants who have lived since the Bible was written.

And there is nothing more helpful to us, in seeking to serve God, than to try and learn the practical lessons which we find illustrated in the lives of the good and holy men, who have been a blessing to the church and to the world through their faithful labors.

The "Heroes of the Reformation" belong to this class, and these sketches of their noble lives are sent forth in the earnest hope that through God's blessing they may prove useful to the young who are trying to serve him. R. N.

CONTENTS.

LIST OF ILLUSTRATIONS.

Henry IV. of Germany at Canossa.

HEROES OF THE REFORMATION.

CHAPTER I.

THE EMPEROR OF GERMANY DOING PENANCE. 1077 A. D.

SINCE the founding of the Christian church, and the close of New Testament history, no more important event has ever taken place than the great Reformation. This occurred more than three hundred years ago.

It will be interesting and instructive to talk about some of the great and good men who helped to carry on that great work, and about the events of greatest interest in their lives. Every true American ought to be familiar with the "Heroes and Incidents of the Reformation." In the first two chapters we will present some facts which may give us a view of the real state of religion in the most enlightened countries in the world before the great Reformation. And, therefore, we will speak of the emperor of Germany.

It is not the present emperor, the famous Emperor William, to whom this title refers. It refers to one who was the emperor over eight hundred years ago. Then the church of Jesus Christ in our world was passing through what are called "the dark ages." It was long before the Reformation. Then there was no Protestant branch of the church. The pope of Rome ruled the church everywhere. Both the people and the priests were ignorant, and the church was very corrupt.

The word *penance* is used in describing this scene. This word means something that causes pain. In the church of Rome, when people do what is wrong, the priests require them to do some disagreeable thing, something that will cause them to suffer shame. This is to show sorrow for the wrong they have done. And this, whatever it be, is called *doing penance.*

The emperor of Germany is represented as doing penance in thin clothing, standing barefoot in the snow, and leaning his head against the wall of the castle. If you could take a good look at him, you might think he was some poor beggar, who had been knocking at the gate of the castle and was waiting to get something to eat. But you would make a great mistake in thinking so, for that barefooted man was Henry IV., the emperor of Germany. Now, there are two questions that we may ask about this:

1. *How did the emperor come into this position?* He had been quarrelling with the pope of Rome. At that time Gregory VII. was pope. He was a very proud and ambitious man. He was not satisfied to be the head of the church, as the popes called themselves, but wanted also to be the head and master of all the kingdoms of the world. He wanted to take away

from the emperor and other rulers some of the rights and privileges which had always belonged to them. This made the emperor very angry. He thought that the pope was interfering with things that did not belong to him. And he was right in thinking so. But the pope would not mind what the emperor said. He was determined to have his own way. Henry was unwilling to submit to this. So he called a great council or convention at the city of Worms. This council passed a resolution that Gregory should be deposed or put out of his office, and that another pope should be chosen. This made Gregory very angry. In order to punish the emperor, he declared that he was excommunicated, or put out of the church. This meant not only that he was not to be allowed to come to the communion any more, but also that he was not to be emperor any longer, and that the people were not to obey his laws, or to mind what he said, or pay any attention to him. If the pope should attempt to do this to-day, the people would only laugh at it;

nobody would mind it. But it was very different then. Everybody was afraid of the pope. Henry soon found that the pope was too strong for him. He saw that unless he made up with the pope, and got him to withdraw the sentence of excommunication, he was likely to lose his empire. And so in the midst of winter he took a long journey, with only his wife and a few servants, to see the pope, and ask pardon for what he had done. When he came to the castle at Canossa, in Lombardy, where Gregory was living, the emperor was kept standing out in the cold three days, before the pope would let him in or have anything to say to him. Then the emperor and the pope made up the quarrel, and Henry went home to exercise the power that belonged to him.

2. *What may we learn from this story?* It shows us very clearly how much there is in the church of Rome that is different from the church which Jesus established! One day when Jesus was on earth, a man came to him and said, "Master, speak to my brother that he divide the inheritance

with me. And Jesus said to him, Man, who made me a judge or a divider over you?" (Luke 12 : 13, 14). On another occasion Jesus said, "My kingdom is not of this world" (John 18 : 36). But the popes of Rome have always been ready to do what Jesus refused to do. They will divide not only private inheritances, but crowns and kingdoms. Jesus never undertook to mingle with politics, or arbitrarily to control crowns and kings. But the popes have always been glad enough to do these things. And this shows how different the church of Rome is from the church of Jesus!

And then this story shows us *how thankful we should be for the Reformation.* It was not until the Reformation that the popes began to lose their worldly power. Since then they have been gradually losing it more and more. And now, in our own day, the pope has lost all the power that he and the other popes used to have as *worldly* princes. And we as Protestants have reason to rejoice over this. If it had not been for the Reformation such scenes as we have described might still be taking place. The more people read the Bible for themselves, the more plainly they will see how different the church of Rome is from the church which Jesus founded.

CHAPTER II.

KING JOHN AND THE POPE'S LEGATE.

1199–1216.

THIS is a well-known incident in English history. As England is our mother country, it is natural for us to feel an interest in her history. The event referred to took place in the reign of King John. It is nearly seven hundred years since the reign of John. He began his reign in the year 1199, the last year of the twelfth century, and reigned through the first sixteen years of the thirteenth century. This seems like a long way back. It is about one-third of the whole time since our Saviour came upon the earth.

In relating this story there are three things to speak of.

1. *A proud priest.* Imagine a priest sitting in a chair on a platform. He is

what is called the legate, or ambassador of the pope of Rome. At the time to which we refer, Innocent III. was the pope. He was one of the proudest and most powerful of all the popes. It is of him we now speak as the proud priest. The legate was only speaking and acting for his master the pope. He might well be called the proud priest. This pope had a quarrel with John, king of England. At first the king resisted the pope. He declared the pope's legate should "at his peril set his foot on the soil of England." Then the pope pretended to take away his crown. He told the king's subjects not to obey him. He would not allow the king, or the princes, or the people, to have any churches open, or to hold any religious services. The doors of the churches were watched; the people were driven from them like dogs; the dead were refused Christian burial; there was deep sadness over the whole land. So an old writer tells us. This frightened the king. He asked the pope's pardon. And when the poor king came on his knees before the pope's legate, and humbly begged permission to wear his crown, he coolly kicked it aside. This was a proud priest indeed! He claimed to be the servant and representative of Christ. *This* was not acting like the meek and gentle Jesus. And the Bible tells us that "If any man have *not* the spirit of Christ, he is none of his" (Rom. 8 : 9).

2. *A weak king.* Such a king was John, the king of England. He began a quarrel with the pope. That proud priest was not only claiming the highest authority over the church in England, but over the kingdom. He wanted to have the power to appoint the Archbishop of Canterbury, who is the highest officer in the church of England; and also to decide who should be the king, and sit upon the throne.

This was something very important to the king of England, and to the people also. It was something worth fighting for. It was no wonder that John refused, at first, to agree that the pope should have any such power as this. It was not worth while to be a king, or to have a crown, on these terms. It was right for John to oppose the pope, when he claimed to have such a right as this over the church and the government of England. But John showed his weakness in giving up the struggle so soon. He agreed to let the pope have his own way. He admitted the pope's right to give him his crown or to take it away from him whenever he might please to do so. He basely kneeled down before the pope's servant, and begged permission to wear the crown of England. Shame! shame on John! Truly he *was* a weak king! This is one of the most disgraceful things that any king of England ever did.

It is pleasant to turn away from this view, and think of

3. *A brave people.* The people of England were very angry at what their poor weak king had done. They were not willing that their liberty as a people should be handed over to a foreigner. They would not consent that the man who happened to be the pope of Rome should have the power to rule their church and

their kingdom; to say who should be the Archbishop of Canterbury, or the ruler of their church; and who should be the king of England, or the ruler of their country.

The barons of England, who were the princes of those days, and represented the people, had a meeting. They made the king appoint a meeting between himself and them. This meeting was on the meadow of Runnymede or an island in the river Thames. There the king was obliged to take back what he had promised to the pope, and to make a covenant or agreement that would secure to the English people those liberties which he had weakly given away. This agreement was called "The Magna Charta," or the *Great Charter*. This was a great blessing to England. John died at Newark Castle in 1216, after suffering great loss in trying to cross a shallow bay called the Wash. And thus as we remember this great event in English history, we may think of three things: the *proud priest*, the *weak king*, and the *brave people*.

Ludgarshall Church, where Wycliffe preached, 1368-1374, before he went to Lutterworth.

Lutterworth Church, where Wycliffe preached at the time of his death.

CHAPTER III.

JOHN WYCLIFFE. 1320–1384.

FOREMOST among the Reformers stands John de Wycliffe. He was not really one of the Reformers himself, but was one of the first to prepare the way for the Reformation. You know that before the sun rises in the morning, to drive away the darkness of the night, we often have a bright, particular star, shining beautifully in the eastern sky. We call it the "morning star." It comes to tell us that the sun is going to rise. The Reformation was like the sun rising on the church after the long night of "the dark ages." And Wycliffe was "the morning star of the Reformation." In considering the life of this great man we may speak

1. *Of his birth and residence.* He was born at a village called Wycliffe, near the

town of Richmond, in Yorkshire, about 1324 or possibly as early as 1320. It was about two hundred years before the Reformation took place. His Christian name was John. Hardly any two persons spell his name in the same way. It has been spelled in not less than twenty-eight (one says fifty) different ways. The two ways most common abroad are *Wiclif*, preferred by Lechler, who wrote a life of the Reformer, and *Wyclif*, used by the Wyclif society. In America the more common spelling is *Wycliffe*, and this is the way the name of the hamlet and of "Wycliffe Hall" in Oxford is spelled; the Wy pronounced long.* If any of our young

* The following forms of spelling this name are said to be in use: Wiclif, Wicliv, Wiclef, Wiclyf, Wicleff, Wicliff, Wiclyff, Wiclyve, Wicliffe, Wicklif, Wicklef, Wickleff, Wickliff, Wickliffe, Wickleffe, Wicklyf, Wiyclif, Wigclif, Wyclif, Wyclef, Wyclife, Wyclefe, Wyclyf, Wycleff, Wycliff, Wyclyff, Wyclyfe, Wyclyffe, Wycliffe, Wyclyve, Wycklef, Wyckliff, Wyckliffe, Wycklyffe, Wycleve, Wycluffe, Wyccliff, Wyccylff Witcliffe, Whitcliff, Whytclyfe, Whyteclyve, Wykeclyfe, Vuiclif, Vuiclevus, Vuythclyffus, Wiclefus, Wicleflus, Wicleffius, Wicklefus, Wicoclivus. So while we honor "the morning star of the Reformation," we cannot tell which is the most accurate way to spell his name.—E. W. R.

readers do not like the way in which it is spelled here they can take their choice out of the other ways.

He studied at Oxford. After entering the ministry he was settled in three different places. The last of these was the little town of Lutterworth. Here he spent the last ten years of his life, and this is the place with which his name is chiefly connected. This is a small market town in the central part of England, about eighty miles from London. It stands on a hill overlooking the Swift, a little stream, which runs into the Avon. The chief thing of interest about the place, is that Wycliffe lived and labored here. The same church and the same pulpit in which he preached are here still. The church is a large, stone building, quite handsomely fitted up in the interior, with the portrait of Wycliffe hanging up in it. The table and gown which he used are also shown to visitors. Our country is so new that we hardly know how we should feel in visiting a church that had been worshipped in for *more than five hundred years!*

2. *Wycliffe's work.* His work was of three kinds. And he was a great worker in each of these kinds. He was great as a *preacher*. He studied the Bible very carefully. He loved to preach the gospel. And he did this with a clearness, and faithfulness, and power that was unusual in those days. Crowds came to hear him. His great piety gave power to what he said. And in addition to preaching himself, he trained up a large number of men to help him in this work. These men went all over the country preaching the gospel in churchyards, at fairs, in market places, by the wayside, and wherever they could get people to come and hear them. In this way he did a wonderful amount of good.

And he was a *great debater*, as well as a preacher. The monks, and priests, and friars of the Romish church went about the country teaching the people all sorts of wrong doctrines. He disputed bravely with these men whenever he met with them. Besides contending with them himself, he wrote a great number of tracts, which were written out, and scattered abroad to guard the people against their errors.*

On one occasion he was taken very ill, and it was thought he was going to die. Some of the "begging Friars" came to see him. He had said a great many very severe things against them. They asked him to take back all that he had said against them before he died. He listened to what they had to say; then he made signs for his attendants to raise him in his bed. Fixing his eyes on the friars he stretched forth his hand and said: "I shall not die, but live and declare the errors and sins of you wicked men more than ever."

But Wycliffe's *greatest work, after all, was his translation of the Scriptures.* Before his time there had been no translation of the Bible made into the English

* Professor Shirley in a catalogue names ninety-six Latin works, and sixty-five English works by Wycliffe. His published sermons number two hundred and ninety-seven. Copies of all these works are still in existence. Besides these Prof. Shirley gives the titles of forty-six works of Wycliffe now lost.—E. W. R.

language. Some parts of it had been translated. But he went earnestly to work, and kept on working, till the whole of God's blessed word had been written out for the people of England in their own language. This was a great work. It was what an angel from heaven would have been glad to do. True, printing was not then known; and the Bibles used had to be written out slowly by the pen, instead of being multiplied rapidly by the press. Still it was a glorious work which Wycliffe did in this matter, and more than anything else it helped to prepare the way for the Reformation.*

* Wycliffe's translation of the Bible was made from the Latin or Vulgate, and not from the original Hebrew and Greek. Of the first translation by him, only about 15 to 18 copies are now known to be in existence. He undertook to revise his translation, aided by a trusty friend and scholar, John Purvey, and of the revised version more than 150 copies are still preserved. A Bible in those days was an expensive book. "Poor people gathered their pennies and formed co-partneries for the purchase of the sacred volume. Those who could afford it gave a sum equal to about $200 for a manuscript copy; others for a few leaves of Peter or Paul would give a load of hay."

The version is in quaint old English, and the letters are as quaint as the style. It may interest many readers who cannot readily find specimens of this old translation, to see a para-

3. *Wycliffe's trials.* These were many and great. The times in which he lived were very unsettled and troublesome. The Roman Catholic bishops, and other leading persons in that church, disliked him very much for preaching and writing against their errors. They tried to worry

graph taken from it. The type is modern, but the spelling is that of the old translation. It is Wycliffe's version of the healing of the cripple at the pool of Bethesda. John. 5: 2-10.

"And in ierusalem is a waischynge place/ that in ebrewe is named bethsaida/ and hath fyue porchis/ in these laie a greete multitude of sike men/ blinde/ crokid/ and drie/ abidynge the mouynge of the watir/ for the aungel of the lord cam doun certeyn tymes in to the watir/ and the watir was moued/ and he that first cam doun in to the sistterne aftir the mouynge of the watir was made hool of what euer sikenesse he was holden/ and a man was there hauynge eiyte and thritti yeer in his sikenesse/ and whanne ihesus hadde seen hym liggynge and hadde knowen/ that he hadde myche tyme/ he seith to him/ wolt thou be made hool/ the sike man answerid to hym/ lord I haue no man that whanne the water is moued to putte me in to the cisterne/ for the while I come/ another goith doun bifor me.

"Ihesus seith to hym/ rise up/ take thi bed and go/ and anoon the man was made hool/ and took up his bedde and wente forth/ and it was saboth in that dai."

The reader will notice the absence of capitals; the varied forms of spelling the same word, as "him" and "hym," "bed" and "bedde," and that "u" takes the place of "v" in most words; facts which show how new the English tongue was in those days.—E. W. R.

him all they could. They brought many charges against him, and had him tried a number of times, for contradicting the doctrines of their church. They wished very much to get the authorities to stop him from preaching, and to have him imprisoned, or put to death. But all the bishops and cardinals, with the pope at their head, were never able to do this. And the reason was, that God raised up very warm friends for Wycliffe among the nobility of England. These men always stood by him when he was brought up by his enemies for trial, and never would allow them to do him any harm. And so, in spite of all his trials and persecutions, he lived on till he reached the age of sixty or sixty-five years.

4. *His death and his disciples.* He died in the year 1384. He was conducting service, one day in his church at Lutterworth, when he was seized with paralysis. The attack was so severe that he was unable to speak, and was utterly helpless. He continued in this state for two days, and then died a calm and gentle death. We sometimes hear it said that, "God buries his

workmen, but carries on his work." It was so with Wycliffe. A large number of good and faithful men, who had become his disciples, went about everywhere, preaching the same doctrines that he had preached, and trying to lead men to know, and love, and serve Jesus.

He was buried in the graveyard connected with his church at Lutterworth. About forty-four years after his death, his enemies dug up his bones, burnt them to ashes, and threw the ashes into the Swift. Thomas Fuller quaintly said, "thus this brook hath conveyed his ashes into Avon; Avon into Severn; Severn into the narrow seas: they into the main ocean. And thus the ashes of Wickliffe are the emblem of his doctrine, which now is dispersed all the world over." The poet Wordsworth puts the same thought thus:

"As thou these ashes, little brook, wilt bear
Into the Avon—Avon to the tide
Of Severn—Severn to the narrow seas—
Into the main ocean they—this deed accurst
An emblem yields to friends and enemies
How the bold teacher's doctrine. sanctified
By truth, shall spread throughout the world dispersed."

CHAPTER IV.

JOHN HUSS AND HIS FOLLOWERS.

1369–1415.

THE Reformer Wycliffe belonged to England. Now we will go over to the continent of Europe, to notice some of the good men who helped on the Reformation there.

One of the first and most important of these was John Huss. We will speak of the life of Huss; his death; and of his followers.

1. *The life of Huss.* He was born about the year 1370.* The place of his birth was the little town of Hussinetz, Bavaria, in Germany. He studied at Prague, and became a Christian while he was a student, and spent a good deal of

* Lechler says 1369; Gillett and H. B. Smith place his birth in 1373.—E. W. R.

Hussite Preaching.

his time in the study of the scriptures and in reading the works of the great Englishman Wycliffe. This opened his eyes to see the great errors of the Romish church, which was then very corrupt.

As soon as he finished his studies and was ordained, he began to preach and write very earnestly against all the wrong things that he saw in the church of Rome. He preached with so much clearness and power that multitudes of people, in all that part of the country were set to thinking and talking about these matters. The friends of the church of Rome became alarmed. A public meeting was called for the purpose of condemning the doctrines of Wycliffe. Huss and his friends tried to prevent this, but they did not succeed. Two parties were now formed. One of these was made up of the friends of Huss and of his doctrines, and the other of the friends of the pope and the church of Rome. This took place in the year 1403, and was the beginning of the Reformation in that part of the world.

The Roman bishops tried to stop Huss from preaching, but the queen of Bavaria was his friend, and attended his church, and she and her husband protected him. The bishops wrote to the pope charging Huss with being a heretic, or a man who did not believe the truth. The pope told them to forbid Huss from preaching and to destroy his books. So they got together a great pile of two hundred writings of Huss and Wycliffe, and made a bonfire of them. But Huss continued to preach and plenty more books were found, so that in spite of all the efforts of the pope and the bishops the good work went on.

2. *The death of Huss.* When the pope found that these Reformed doctrines were spreading rapidly, he tried to stop them in another way. He wrote to the emperor of Germany, and told him to call a great council of bishops and learned men, to meet at the city of Constance for the purpose of trying Huss. The emperor ordered him to appear before this council. The friends of Huss would not let him go, till the emperor gave him what was called

"a safe conduct," that is, a promise that he should not be hurt there, but should be protected, and allowed to return in safety, whatever the result of his trial might be. Relying on this promise of the emperor, Huss went to the council. But the friends of the pope persuaded the emperor to break his word. They told him that it was no sin to break a promise made to what they called a heretic. The emperor was weak enough, and wicked enough to mind them. He withdrew his promise. Huss was put in prison, loaded with chains, and finally burnt to death.

If it is right to judge of a tree by the fruit it bears, what should we think of a religion that teaches men deliberately to break their most solemn promises?

3. *The Hussites, or followers of Huss.* When their leader was killed, his friends whom he had taught, took up his work, and carried it on. He left a large number of followers.* Our picture represents

* One of the noblest of his co-laborers and followers was Jerome of Prague. Jerome was born of a noble family about 1365, and was burned at the stake for his religion in

one of them preaching the gospel to a company of people, out in the open air. The preacher holds a goblet in his right hand. This refers to one of the points of difference between the Romanists and the Reformers. When our Saviour established the Lord's Supper, he commanded all to eat the bread, which represented his body, and to drink the wine, which represented his blood. The Romish church would not let any but the priests take the cup and drink the wine. But Huss and his followers insisted on having both. This is the meaning of the cup in the hands of the preacher.

1416 in the same place as Huss. Huss was the more powerful character; Jerome the more eloquent orator; Huss had the stronger will, the greater endurance in daily toil; Jerome had the keener intellect, the profounder learning. Jerome studied at Oxford and brought home the writings of Wycliffe, and suffered martyrdom for his religion, with great composure and even joy. As the flames crept about him, he repeated a portion of the Apostle's Creed, and sang the Easter hymn, "Salve festa dies," "Hail, festal day." Huss and Jerome had many followers, who were called Hussites, but they refused this title and wanted to be known as Catholic Christians—but not Roman Catholics.—E. W. R.

CHAPTER V.

GIROLAMO SAVONAROLA. 1452–1498.

THERE is a beautiful picture of this great man. He stands erect and appears to be actively engaged in his life work as a preacher of the gospel. Judging from this picture we should naturally think of Savonarola as a very tall man; but this was not the case, he is said to have been a man of medium stature. The impression of him which the picture makes is owing to the long, straight robe which he wore. This would make even a short man look tall.

The *facts* in the life of Savonarola, briefly stated are: he was born at Ferrara in Italy on the twenty-first of September, 1452. This was more than a quarter of a century before the birth of Luther. The family to which he belonged was one of great respectability and honor. His education was carefully conducted. It was intended that he should study medicine and be a physician; but his early religious development led him in another direction. At the age of seventeen he entered a monastery and spent years in diligent study. Then he was ordained to the ministry, and went about from place to place, preaching the gospel with wonderful simplicity and power. The city of Florence was the principal scene of his labors. There he had immense congregations to listen to him. He preached boldly against all the evils that prevailed, at that time, both in the church and among the clergy, as well as in the world. He persuaded the people to bring their costly and useless ornaments to him, and he made a bonfire of them.* A rich lady

* Savonarola was remarkably successful in carrying reforms into the home and child-life of the Florentines. He induced the young to give up their indecent behaviour and savage amusements at carnivals, and to sing hymns and psalms instead of foul songs. He used to preach to vast audiences of children in the great amphitheatre of the Duomo, or cathedral. He was a mediæval Anthony Comstock; for, to purify

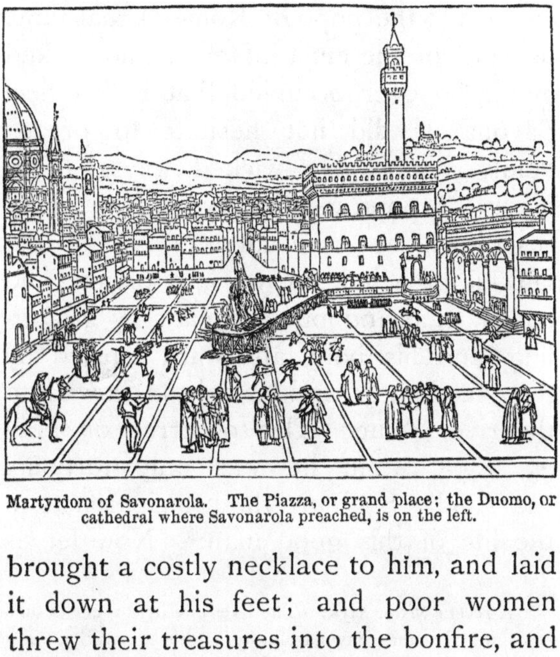

Martyrdom of Savonarola. The Piazza, or grand place; the Duomo, or cathedral where Savonarola preached, is on the left.

brought a costly necklace to him, and laid it down at his feet; and poor women threw their treasures into the bonfire, and then humbly showed reverence for God's minister by kissing the hem of his robe.

He continued his labors for years with great success. He was not afraid to rebuke sin wherever he saw it. Alex-

the city of Florence, he persuaded the people to make a great bonfire of all the obscene pictures, books, dresses, and masks that could be gathered together. The vast pile so consumed is said to have been worth 22,000 florins.—E. W. R.

ander VI., the pope of Rome at that time, was one of the most infamous and wicked men who ever occupied that high office. Savonarola did not hesitate to preach boldly against his wicked ways. This made the pope very angry, and he never rested till he succeeded in having the faithful preacher thrown into prison, and finally tried and put to death by strangling, and his body afterward burned by the executioner, and his ashes thrown into the river Arno. This occurred on May 23, 1498, when he was only forty-six years old. Such are the principal facts in the life of this good man.* Now let us

* A recent writer says: "The lives of Christopher Columbus and Girolamo Savonarola were almost parallel. The latter was born when Columbus was still a very small boy, dreaming, perhaps, even then of the worlds unknown, as he looked wonderingly on the crowded port of his native Genoa. Columbus married a few years before Savonarola entered the cloister, and they may both be said to have begun their life work at the same time. . . . Then both passed through a period of neglect and opposition. . . . For the next few years (after the discovery of America) the influence of Columbus was great and every honor was shown him. It was at the same period that Savonarola was at the zenith of his influence and fame: but the great discoverer, like the prophet-tribune, was to have his name and his honor dragged

look at some of the lessons we may learn from his life.

1. *The good that results from the right use of the Bible.* The fifteenth century, in which Savonarola lived, was one of those that we call the "dark ages." The Bible was very little known and very little preached in those days. A man might go to church for years then, and never find out what the Bible said he must do to be saved. The priests knew very little about the Bible, and of course what they did not know themselves they could not teach to others. But Savonarola came preaching the glorious gospel of Jesus in a plain, simple way, which the people could understand and which won their hearts. And what made the difference between his preaching and that of others in his day? Where did he get the light which others never had? He got it from the Bible. When he was a student he used to read

through the mire. . . . Like Savonarola he was ever pursued by jealous and treacherous foes. . . . Age of Columbus and Savonarola, of Richard III. and Alexander III! What contrasts of light and darkness."—E. W. R.

the Bible carefully and prayerfully every day. He committed it nearly all to memory. This was the sun which gave him light. Here he learned the way of salvation. Here he saw that his great duty as a minister was to know nothing else among men save Jesus Christ and him crucified. It was his earnest study of the Bible that made Savonarola the useful and successful minister that he was. And if we hope to be successful in working for God and for our fellow men, we must follow his example and learn the lesson he has set us of making a right use of the Bible.

2. *The necessity of patient effort in order to great success in our life work.* When Savonarola first began to preach, no one who heard him once cared to hear him again. He did not know how to use his voice, nor how to speak in a way that would be interesting and attractive to his hearers. He was awkward in his gestures, violent in his manner, and crowded his sermons with a profusion of figures and imagery, which excited ridicule. Now

under these circumstances many a young man would have been discouraged and would have said to himself, "Well, it's not worth while for me to try any more; people won't come to hear me. I may as well give up the idea of being a preacher, and turn my thoughts to something else." But Savonarola did not do this; he felt sure that God had called him to preach the gospel, and that whatever hindrances were in his way, he must try to overcome. And this is just what he did. He began patiently and perseveringly to study the art of speaking. He got the best instructions about it that he could get. Then he applied those instructions to his own case. He found out what his faults were, then he tried to correct them, and kept on trying till he succeeded. And this is a most important lesson for us all to learn. It is only by patient, persevering effort that we can hope to succeed in any great and good work. God's promise to each of us is, "I will help thee." But God only helps those who try to help themselves, as Savonarola did in his work as a preacher. Just here the old fable of the man with the stalled wagon comes in. When he found his wagon stalled in the rut, he hoped to get it out by prayer alone; but the voice from heaven told him that he must put his shoulder to the wheel and start up the horses, as well as call on God for help, if he hoped to get out of his trouble. This was what Savonarola did, and this is what we must do if we hope for success in our life work.*

* Savonarola's firmness for the truth, and his resolute will, are finely illustrated in his interview with Lorenzo de Medici. Lorenzo was sick unto death. He was wealthy, powerful, with keen discernment of character. He took large draughts of distilled precious stones, prescribed for his recovery, but to no purpose. He needed a confessor, but had no faith in the sincerity of his priest. He suddenly thought of the prior, Savonarola, and said: "He is the only honest man, send for him." Savonarola came: he required three things of the dying de Medici: 1. Faith in Christ—to this Lorenzo readily assented; 2. To restore all that had been unjustly taken—at this he was surprised and grieved, but finally assented; 3. To restore liberty to the people of Florence. The dying prince turned scornfully on his bed without a word, and Savonarola left the dying man without absolution. —E. W. R.

Boyhood of Luther.

CHAPTER VI.

MARTIN LUTHER, AS A BOY. 1483–1496.

WE have spoken already of three great and good men who may well be put among the "Heroes of the Reformation." These are Wycliffe, Huss, and Savonarola. Yet these men were not so much reformers themselves, as persons whom God used to help in preparing the way for the Reformation.

You remember how it was when our Saviour was coming into the world, John the Baptist was sent as the messenger to prepare the way for his great work.

You know how it is with the morning when it comes. We do not pass at once from the darkness of night to the brightness of day. The morning dawns very gradually upon us. First, the day star appears and tells us that the sun is coming.

Then we begin to see a very faint streak of light in the east, just where the earth and sky seem to meet together. As we watch it the light increases. The sky grows brighter and brighter, till at last the sun rises and shines forth in all his glory.

And it is just so with all the great works that God carries on. He seems to do his work slowly. He is never in a hurry. As the Bible tells us, "He inhabiteth eternity." So he has plenty of time for carrying on all his works. And this is what the prophet means when he says, "His going forth is prepared as the morning" (Hosea 6 : 3). As the sun rises gradually to give us light and warmth in the world, so—in the same gradual way—God prepares and carries on all his works in our world.

And this was the way in which the Reformation was brought about. There was a long time spent in preparing for it. And Wycliffe, Huss, Jerome of Prague, Savonarola, and other good men God used in this work of preparation. And if we call them the morning stars of the Reformation, we may well call Luther the sun of the bright day that then began to shine on the world and on the church.

In speaking of the other "Heroes of the Reformation," we have only given one chapter to each of them. But there is so much to say about Luther that we shall have to take several chapters, so as to bring out the most important points of his life. In the present one we wish to speak of *the birth* and *the boyhood* of Luther.

1. *The birth of Luther.* The great Reformer Luther, was born in a small town called Eisleben. It is situated in that part of Germany known as Saxony.* Like Nazareth, where Jesus was brought up, it had never been distinguished for any great event before. But now, it will

* Eisleben is on the railway from Leipsic to Cassel, by way of Nordhausen and the old town of Halle. Halle is on the River Saale about 25 miles northwest of Leipsic. About 10 miles west of Halle, after crossing a fertile plain, the road passes between sheets of water, one fresh and another salt, and ranges of hills, and in 10 miles more reaches Eisleben, once the capital of Mansfield district. For a graphic description of the town and the scenery about it, see Sears' "Life of Luther," Chap. I.—E. W. R.

always be honor enough for that town, to have it known that Martin Luther was born there. The date of his birth was November 10, 1483. This is over four hundred years ago. The very house in which he was born is still standing, though it is now used as a school for orphans. The church in which he was baptized is standing also, and the font in which his baptism took place is preserved. He was named Martin because the day on which he was born, was called in the Romish church St. Martin's day. Luther spent his last days in the place where he was born, and the pulpit in which he preached his last sermon is shown to travellers, and so is the house in which he died.

But now let us look, for a moment, at

2. *The boyhood of Luther.* His parents were poor. They were miners. Shortly after his birth they moved from Eisleben to Mansfield. Luther's father made up his mind to give his son Martin, a good education. But the poor boy had a pretty hard time in getting it. The teachers of that day were very severe. They believed

that beating boys was the best way to make them learn.* Poor Martin had fifteen whippings in a single day's session at one of his schools. I wonder he ever learned anything at this rate. The boys of that day used to help pay the expenses of their schooling by going around at Christmas holidays singing Christmas carols, for which the people gave them money. This is what Luther did in his school-boy days.†

* Remembering his experience he speaks of some teachers, "who hurt noble minds by their vehement storming, beating, and pounding, wherein they treat children as a jailer doth convicts." Again he declares: "The schools were purgatories, and the teachers were tyrants and task-masters."—E. W. R.

† Luther tells us how when a lad he was wont to go out with companions begging for support while at school. "At Christmas, during divine service, we went around among small villages, singing from house to house, in four parts, as we were wont, the hymn on the child Jesus born in Bethlehem." One peasant, before whose hut they sang, came out, and in the coarse, harsh manner of the peasants, offered them some sausages. This so terrified the boys that they scampered away.—E. W. R.

CHAPTER VII.

MARTIN LUTHER IN YOUTH. 1497–1510

We have spoken of Luther's *birth* and *boyhood.* We will look at him now, *as a student* and *a priest.*

1. *Luther as a student.* From Mansfield young Luther was sent to Magdeburg to continue his studies. There his privations and hardships were so great that his father took him from Magdeburg to Eisenach, where he studied for four years. The famous castle of Wartburg is near this town; a castle distinguished as the hiding place of Luther after the Diet of Worms. When he was eighteen years of age he went to the university in the town of Erfurth, and began to study law. Here he spent about seven years in study. He was very quick in learning and soon became one of the best scholars in the

Luther on the Holy Staircase, Rome.

university. His father was very proud of him, and resolved to give him the best education he could have. He knew it would cost a great deal of money, but he was quite willing to pay this, because he thought that Martin would become a great lawyer and be famous for his learning.

After finishing his daily lessons, instead of spending his time in company, as most young men did, he used to go into the library, and occupy himself in reading. While doing this he found one day a copy of the Latin Bible. It was the first time he had ever seen a Bible. How strange this seems to us! He had heard portions of scripture read by priests in church, and he thought that those were all the Bible. He read that Bible with great interest, and felt as if he would gladly give all he had in the world to have a copy of the whole Bible as his own.* But

* The old German chronicler Mathesius tells us, that in turning over the leaves of this old Latin Bible Luther's eye fell upon the history of Samuel and his mother Hannah. This he quickly read through with joy and delight, and it was probably the first portion of scripture Luther ever read. —E. W. R.

books were very scarce, and it was impossible for him to get one of them.

Not long after this, Luther made up his mind to give up the study of law, and to study theology, in order to become a priest. Two things happened to him which led him to make this change. One of these was the sudden death of a young friend and fellow student, whom he loved very much. It is uncertain whether he was killed by violence, or whether he died from disease; but he died very suddenly. When Luther heard of it, he said to himself, "What would become of me, if I should die as suddenly." This was one thing that led him to think of becoming a priest.

About the same time, while walking in the country he was overtaken by a violent storm. When the storm burst, a thunderbolt fell almost at his feet. This startled him greatly. He made a vow on the spot that he would change his life and become a priest. He did so at once. His friends were surprised. His father was displeased. But he felt it was the right thing for him to do, and he did it.

Then he left the university where he had been studying law and entered a monastery. This was a building occupied by men called monks. These men lived by themselves, and professed to be very religious. After going through his studies here, the time came for him to enter on the work which he had chosen.

2. *Luther as a priest.* He was ordained to this office in the year 1507. He was then about twenty-one years of age. He began at once to do all the good he could by visiting the poor, and teaching and preaching to them as well as he knew how. Within a year of his ordination he was invited by Frederic, Prince of Saxony, to move to the town of Wittenberg and become one of the teachers or professors in the university in that place. He went and soon became famous as a teacher in the university, and as a preacher, both there and through the surrounding country. Still at this time he was only a priest in the corrupt church of Rome. He did not yet understand the gospel of Jesus.

The old Augustinian cloister (Luther's home) at Wittenberg. His room was in the second story (second and third windows from the right).

One thing that opened Luther's eyes to see the great errors of the church of Rome, and led him to become a true Christian and a Reformer, was a visit that he made to the great city of Rome in 1510. This, you know, is where the pope lives, and here are the headquarters of the Romish church. When he came here Luther expected to find the church very pure and the priests all good and holy men. But in this he was greatly disappointed. He found that Rome was one of the wickedest places he had ever seen. The church was full of all sorts of errors and evil practices. The priests were, most of them, bad men, who did not seem to believe the things they were teaching to the people.

In a chapel connected with one of the principal churches in Rome, there was then, and there is still, a flight of white marble steps, called the "Scala Sancta," or "Holy Stairs." The priests said that these stairs were the very ones up which our Saviour walked when he was going from Pilate's judgment hall to Calvary, and that an angel had brought them from Jerusalem to Rome. The people were told that whoever went up these stairs on their knees would have all their sins forgiven. Luther began to go up these steps on his knees. But when he was part of the way up, it seemed to him as if he heard a loud voice saying, "*The just shall live by faith.*" This made him start. He rose from his knees and went away. This was a sort of turning point in Luther's history. It had a great effect on his mind, and helped to prepare him for the great events in his life.

CHAPTER VIII.

LUTHER BURNS THE POPE'S BULL. 1520.

This was a very important event in the life of the great Reformer, Martin Luther. You remember that as he was going up what are called "the holy stairs" at Rome he started, when about half way up, because he seemed to hear a voice saying to him, "*The just shall live by faith.*" That, as we said, was a turning point in Luther's life. From that time his views of religion became clearer than ever they had been before. If you look through a window of stained glass you can see nothing plainly. But if you look through a clear glass window you can see everything distinctly. Up to that time Luther's mind had been like a stained or glazed window, and all his views of the gospel of Jesus were dim and cloudy. But then his mind became

The market place at Wittenberg—on the left, the City Hall—in the centre, the City Church where Luther was accustomed to preach—and in front, Luther's monument.

clear, and for the first time in his life he began to understand what the gospel is, and how men are saved by it.

Now we come to a second turning point in Luther's history. The first referred to a great change that took place in his *thoughts and feelings;* but this refers to a change that took place in his *life and actions.*

1. *What is meant by the Pope's Bull?* You know that in the fall of every year, the President of the United States publishes a letter to all the people of this country, appointing a particular day, generally the last Thursday in November, as a day of public thanksgiving to God, for all his mercies to us. This letter is called the president's *proclamation.* And so the pope of Rome sometimes sends out a letter, or proclamation to the people belonging to his church, in all parts of the world. In this letter he tells them to do, or not to do certain things; to believe, or not to believe certain doctrines. And this letter or proclamation of the pope is called his "bull." This name comes from the

Latin word "bulla," which means a seal. The pope's proclamation always has a great seal, made of lead or gold. On the side of this seal, the heads of the apostles Peter and Paul are stamped; and on the other the name of the pope. This seal is fastened to the letter by a ribbon or cord. And then, because that letter has the pope's seal fastened to it, the name of that seal is given to the letter itself, and it is called "the pope's bull."

2. *What led Luther to burn the Pope's Bull?* He had been very much grieved by the errors which the Romish priests were teaching, and the wicked things they were doing. Among these, was what was called "the sale of indulgences." An indulgence was a piece of paper or parchment, signed or stamped with the pope's name. This pretended to secure a pardon to any one who bought it. No matter how great the sin was,—whether it was lying, or swearing, or cheating, or stealing, or even murdering; all that a man had to do, was to buy one of these indulgences; and then whether he was sorry for his sin

or not, he was told that he was sure of pardon if he only bought an indulgence. And what was still worse, the priests taught the people that these indulgences would secure them pardon, not only for all the sins they had committed in the past; but also for any sins they might commit in the future.

How dreadful this was! No wonder that Luther was stirred up to preach sermons, and publish tracts and books against these wicked doings. In these, he taught the people that these indulgences were good for nothing; that no one had power to forgive sins but God; and that he would only forgive those who were truly penitent, and had faith in him. These books and writings of Luther were scattered abroad everywhere. This made the pope angry. Then he sent out his letter; or, as they say, "issued his bull." In this he said Luther was a heretic, or one who did not believe the Bible. He said the people must not listen to Luther, nor read his books; but burn them wherever they were found. And so, when Luther got this bull, he called a meeting of his friends, in a public place, had a bonfire made, and threw the pope's bull into it, and burnt it up.

3. *What followed from the burning of Bull?*

THE REFORMATION FOLLOWED.

The pope issued another bull, in which he put Luther out of the church, or as it is called, excommunicated him. This is a big word of six syllables. Before this, Luther expected to remain in the church of Rome. Now he saw that this would be impossible. And then the church of the Reformation was formed.

TETZEL'S INDULGENCE:

TRANSLATED FROM THE LATIN.

[The original is in awkward, stiff Latin, and does not indicate the high order of scholarship sometimes attributed to the court of Leo X.]

"Albert, by the Grace of God, and of the Apostolic See, Archbishop of the Holy See of Mentz and the Church of Magdeburg, Primate and Arch-Chancellor of the Holy Roman Empire in Germany, Prince Elector and Administrator of Halberstadt, Marquis of Brandenburg, of Stettin, of Pomerania, Duke of the Cassabi and the Slaves; Burgrave of Nuremburg, and Prince of Rugen, and Guardian of the Order of Friars Minor of the Observance of the convent of Mentz; Nuncio and Commissary specially deputed for the

Albertus dei et apostolice sedis gratia sancte Moguntinensis sedis ac Magdeburgensis ecclesie Archiepiscopus ...

¶ Forma absolutionis totiens quotiens in vita.

Misereatur tui &c. Dominus noster Jesus christus per meritum sue passionis te absoluat: auctoritate cuius et apostolica mihi in hac parte commissa et tibi concessa: ego te absoluo ab omnibus peccatis tuis. In nomine patris et filij et spiritus sancti Amen.

Forma absolutionis et plenissime remissionis: semel in vita et in mortis articulo.

Misereatur tui &c. Dominus noster Jesus christus per meritum sue passionis te absoluat: et ego auctoritate ipsius et apostolica mihi in hac parte commissa et tibi concessa te absoluo. Primo ab omni sententia excommunicationis maioris vel minoris si quam incurristi. Deinde ab omnibus peccatis tuis: conferendo tibi plenissimam omnium peccatorum tuorum remissionem, remittendo tibi etiam penas purgatorii in quantum se claues sancte matris ecclesie extendunt. In nomine patris et filij et spiritus sancti Amen.

FACSIMILE OF THE INDULGENCE PREACHED BY TETZEL.

undermentioned purposes by our most holy lord Pope Leo X. throughout the provinces of Mentz and Magdeburg, and the cities and dioceses thereof, as also those of Halberstadt, likewise the territories and places mediately or immediately subject to the temporal dominion of the most illustrious and illustrious Princes, the Lords Marquises of Brandenburg, to all and singular the faithful shall see the present letters. Health in the Lord. We make known that our most holy lord Leo X., by Divine Providence, now Pope, to all and singular the faithful in Christ of both sexes, who shall extend helping hands towards the reparation of the fabric of the Basilica of the Prince of the Apostles, St. Peter in the City, according to our regulation, beyond those very full indulgences and other graces and faculties which the faithful in Christ may themselves obtain, according to the contents of the Apostolic letters heretofore executed, has also mercifully indulged and granted in the Lord—that they may choose, as a suitable confessor, a secular priest, or a regular of any Mendicant order, who, after diligently hearing their confession, has the power and ability, by Apostolic authority, to plenarily absolve and enjoin salutary penance on them for the faults and excesses committed by the person so choosing him; and from sins of any kind, however grave and enormous; even in cases reserved for the said See; and from ecclesiastical censures, even when undergone by a man at the instance of any one soever, with the consent of the parties; or from those incurred by reason of an interdict, and those the absolution of which has been specially reserved to the said See; except the crimes of conspiracy against the person of the Supreme Pontiff, of the murder of Bishops, or of other superior prelates, and the laying violent hands upon them or other prelates, the forgery of letters Apostolic, the conveying of arms and other prohibited things into heathen countries, and the sentences and censures incurred on occasion of the importation of the alum of Apostolic Tolfa from heathen countries to the faithful, contrary to the Apostolic prohibition; once in life and in the article of death as often as it shall threaten, although death may not then supervene, and in non-reserved cases as often as they shall seek it; and once in life and in the said article of death, to grant plenary indulgence and remissions of all sins; also to commute for other works of piety any vows made by them from time to time (the vows of foreign travel, of visiting the shrines of the Apostles, and of St. James in Compostella, of religion, and of chastity, alone excepted). The same our most holy lord has also granted that the aforesaid benefactors, and their deceased parents who have died in charity, should become partakers for ever in the prayers, suffrages, alms-deeds, fastings, supplications, masses, canonical hours, disciplines, pilgrimages, and all other spiritual benefits which are made and can be made in the universal Holy Church Militant, and in all the members of the same. And, whereas, the devout Philip Kessel, Priest, has shown himself acceptable by contributing of his goods to the fabric itself, and to the necessary restoration of the aforesaid Basilica of the Prince of the Apostles, according to the intention of our most holy lord the Pope, and our ordinance, in sign of which thing he has received from us the present letters; therefore, by the same Apostolic authority committed to us, which we act upon in these parts, we grant and bestow upon him, by these presents the power and ability to use and enjoy the said graces and indulgences. Given at Augsburg, under the seal appointed by us for this purpose, on the 15th day of the month of April, in the year of our Lord 1517.

"Form of Absolution, as often as may be required during life:—

"'Misereatur tui,' &c. (May Almighty God have mercy on thee, forgive thee thy sins, and bring thee to life everlasting.) May our Lord Jesus Christ, by the merit of His Passion absolve thee, by whose authority and that of the Apostolic See, committed to me in these parts and to thee conceded, I absolve thee from all thy sins. In the name of the Father, and of the Son, and of the Holy Ghost. Amen.

"Form of Absolution and fullest remission, once in life and in the article of death.

"'Misereatur tui,' &c. May our Lord Jesus Christ by the merits of His Passion absolve thee, and I, by His authority and that of the Apostolic See, committed to me for this purpose, and to thee conceded, absolve thee, first from every sentence of the greater or lesser excommunication, if thou hast incurred any, and in the next place from all thy sins, by conferring upon thee the fullest remission of all thy sins, and by remitting to thee also the pains of purgatory, so far as the keys of Holy Mother Church extend. In the name of the Father, and of the Son, and of the Holy Ghost. Amen."

This was the indulgence offered for sale by Tetzel, and which Luther opposed with great earnestness. There are some remarkable features in this indulgence to which attention has been directed. Among the sins not admitting of pardon were, "conspiracy against the person of the pontiff, murder of bishops or of other superior prelates," forgery of apostolic (*i. e.*, papal) letters, export of arms to heathen ports, and, most extraordinary of all, "importation of alum contrary to papal direction." The secret of this last exception was, that the pope required all to buy alum imported from Tolfa, which belonged to the pope, and from the sale of this he derived a revenue. Murders by brigands, by secret assassins, for plunder or any purpose could be absolved, if not against a Romish prelate, but the sin of getting alum without the pope's permission could not be forgiven, for it might lessen his pence!—E. W. R.

CHAPTER IX.

LUTHER AT WORMS. 1521.

ONE of the most interesting and important events in the life of the great Reformer Luther, was his trial before the Diet at Worms. The city of Worms, where this great event took place, was an ancient and important city in Germany. The emperors used to reside here. The great emperor Charlemagne was married here. But it has now gone very much to decay. Its present population is about fifteen thousand.*

* Worms is beautifully situated on the Rhine, about 30 miles above Mayence. It was once a flourishing and populous city of 70,000 inhabitants. In an open park or square, stands the imposing monument of Luther which cost £17,000, or $85,000, while an ancient cathedral, having few portions of great antiquity now, stands in the public square, and on its north side is the site of the old Episcopal palace in which Luther made his defence in 1521. The palace was

The word *Diet* was used in Germany to denote a large gathering of men, belonging either to the church or state, brought together to settle some important question connected with the doctrines which are to be believed or the duties that are to be performed. It denoted such a gathering as we should call a convention, or a congress, or an assembly. "The Diet of Worms," then, refers to a famous convention or assembly of this kind, that was held in the city of Worms in the year 1521, or more than three hundred years ago. In speaking of it, there are *three* things to be considered.

1. *Why was it called?* We must remember that at this time the Reformation had been some years in progress. Luther and his friends had been earnestly at work preaching and writing about it. The doctrines of the Bible, as they taught them, were spreading rapidly. Great multitudes of people in Germany, in Switzerland, in

twice destroyed by the French, and on its foundations a beautiful house in more modern style of architecture was erected during the present century.—E. W. R.

France, in England, and other countries of Europe, were leaving the Romish church and joining that of the Reformers. The pope of Rome was getting alarmed. He had been in the habit, when men began to preach as Luther was doing, either of having them cast into prison or put to death in the countries where they lived, or else of summoning them to Rome, and having them burnt as heretics there. But he had not been able to do so with Luther. And the reason was, that God had raised up warm and powerful friends for Luther in some of the great princes of Germany. These men stood by him. They would not let him go to Rome, nor would they let him be put in prison, or be hindered in his work in Germany.

About this time Charles V. was proclaimed emperor of Germany. The pope tried to get his help in putting Luther down. These two men put their heads together, and called a meeting of the Diet of Worms. Luther was summoned to appear before this Diet. The pope and the emperor hoped in this way to do one of two things: either to get Luther to recant, that is, give up the doctrines he had been preaching and publishing, or else to get the authority of this Diet for putting him to death. For this purpose the Diet of Worms was called.

2. *Who were present?* It was one of the grandest assemblies of princes, and rulers, and dignitaries of different kinds, that ever met together. Let us imagine that we have a picture of this great meeting before us. On the extreme right, sitting in a chair, with a crown on his head, and a sceptre in his right hand, is the famous Emperor Charles V. Standing to the right of the emperor, is his brother, the Archduke Ferdinand, in armor, with a drawn sword in his hand. Sitting by a table, in the centre, with a mitre on his head, and a crozier, or bishop's staff, in his hand, is the Archbishop of Treves, who represented the pope on this occasion. On the other side of the table, in a gown and cap, and stretching out his hand, pointing to some books on the table to the left of the picture, is the Chancellor

of the Archbishop, who put the questions to Luther that he was asked on this trial. On the left, standing with head uncovered, looking towards the emperor, and pointing to the table near him, on which lay a number of his books, stands the great Reformer Luther. Standing near him, with his right hand on the handle of his sword, is one of the most powerful of the German princes, and Luther's warmest friend, the Elector of Saxony.

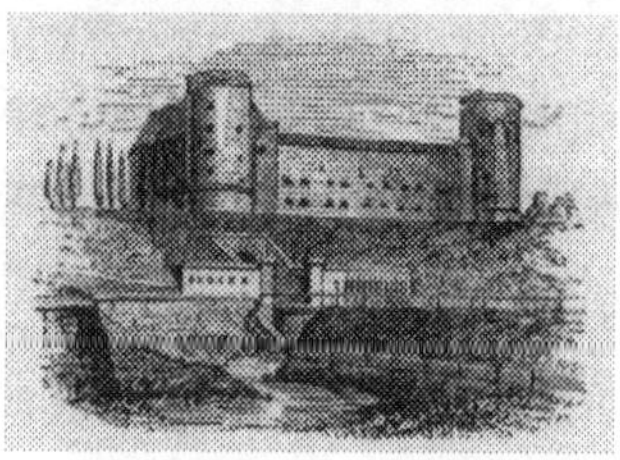

The castle of the Elector at Wittenberg.

Altogether there were present six electors, twenty-four dukes, eight margraves (a title of nobility peculiar to Germany), thirty archbishops, bishops and abbots, seven ambassadors, deputies from ten free cities, the pope's nuncios, and a great number of princes, counts, and sovereign barons; making in all two hundred and four distinguished persons. And then, in addition to these, the great hall in the palace in which the Diet met was filled with a crowd of between four thousand and five thousand people. How grand an assembly this must have been! To a plain man like Luther, who was not accustomed to the presence of kings and the pomp of courts, the whole scene must have been very appalling. Yet he was calm and collected, and never lost his presence of mind.

3. *What was done there?* The noblest testimony to the truth of the gospel ever borne by mortal man was borne by Luther there. When Luther entered, there was great excitement in that vast assembly. Every one in that crowd of five thousand people was anxious to see this famous man. Presently the noise was hushed, and all was still as the grave. Then the Archbishop's chancellor stood up, and said in a loud, clear voice, that there were two questions for Luther to answer. Then

pointing to some books on a table near, he asked Luther "if he was the author of those books?" Luther asked that the titles of them might be read. This was done. Then he said he was the writer of them. The other question asked him was, "Will you retract" (or take back) "everything in them contrary to the teachings of the church of Rome?" Luther asked time for reflection before answering this question. The emperor said he should have till the next day. Then the Diet was adjourned, and met again the following day. Then Luther was called upon for his answer. He made a long speech, first in German and then in Latin. In this he said, that "if it could be proved that anything in his books was contrary to the scriptures, he would at once retract it; but that if this was not done, he could retract nothing." When urged again to retract, he repeated what he had said before, adding, "*Here I stand; I cannot do otherwise. God help me! Amen.*"

As we hear or read about this, we cannot but be struck *with the wonderful courage of Luther!* When he stood up before that vast company of the great ones of the earth, and refused to take back what he had preached or published, it was one of the bravest things that ever man did. As he was about entering that hall, to appear before the emperor, a brave old officer of the army met him, and said to him, "Doctor, what you are now going to do requires a great deal more courage than I ever needed in all the battles I have fought." And this was true. Let us thank God for the courage he gave to Luther, and ask for grace, boldly to "stand up for Jesus" wherever we go.

CHAPTER X.

LUTHER IN WARTBURG CASTLE. 1521.

WE have seen Luther before the Council of Worms, bravely defending his books and doctrines, in the presence of the great emperor, Charles V., and of all the power of the church of Rome. He stood up nobly in defence of what he had preached and printed, and refused to take back or deny anything he had taught, unless they could prove from scripture that it was not true. This made his enemies very angry. They tried to persuade the emperor to have him arrested and put to death. But he had given Luther a "safe conduct" or written promise that he should be allowed to return home in safety. And the emperor was not willing to break his promise. So Luther's enemies were disappointed, and he left the city of Worms unharmed,

Luther entering Wartburg Castle.

to go back to his own home. It was several days' journey then from Worms to Wittenberg, where Luther lived. It is only a few hours journey now by railway. But Luther did not reach his home till nearly a year after he left Worms. He disappeared strangely in the course of the journey, and nothing was heard of him for a long time. His friends were alarmed, and wondered where he was. Some thought he was dead. Others thought that his enemies had caught him and imprisoned him in some dark dungeon, from which he would never come out alive. But they were all mistaken. Luther was a prisoner indeed, yet he was perfectly safe and among kind friends. It turned out after a while that all this time he was in a castle known as Wartburg Castle. This was a strongly fortified castle on the top of a high, rocky hill, in the wildest and most lonely part of a great German forest, known as the Thuringian forest. The present picture represents him as entering this castle. On the right hand side of the picture you see a company of men coming through the gateway. At the head of this company a soldier is seen, leading with his right hand a rather short, stout man; that is Martin Luther. There are several things to consider here.

1. *Who brought Luther into Wartburg Castle?* It was done by his friend, the Elector of Saxony. He was one of the most powerful of the German princes. He was very fond of Luther, and a great friend of the Reformation. When he saw how angry the enemies of Luther were, on account of the victory he had gained over them at the Diet of Worms, he was afraid they would take him prisoner and put him to death as soon as he reached home. And very likely they would have done so. And then this good man made up his mind that he would take Luther prisoner, and keep him hidden away for a while in some unknown place, where he would be safe until the excitement had passed away. So he found out the way which Luther was going to take on his journey home. He sent for a company of horsemen to watch for him

and his friends, in a lonely part of the forest. As Luther and his company were journeying quietly along one day, suddenly a number of horsemen rushed forth upon them. Luther was seized and separated from his friends. They were not hurt; but told to go quietly home, while he was taken away and brought into Wartburg Castle. This is the way Luther got into Wartburg Castle.

2. *What Luther did in Wartburg Castle.* He did several things which were very important and useful. One of these was that he had a good long rest, which he very much needed, because he had been leading such an active, busy life. He was a professor, and had to lecture to the students in the university. He was a minister, and had to preach every Sunday. He was the leader of the Reformation, and had to be going about from place to place, holding arguments with the Romish priests, writing and printing pamphlets, answering all sorts of letters, and like the apostle Paul, having upon him daily "*the care of all the churches.*" And he had

just had one of the hardest trials of his life. Now he had a nice quiet time for studying the Bible, which he did very carefully, in the original Hebrew and Greek languages. This was very useful to him during all the rest of his life. And then after he had been some time in this safe, quiet hiding-place, he began to write letters to his friends in different parts of the country, about the great work in which they were engaged. He used to send these letters by private messengers. And to keep them from knowing where he was, he used to give fanciful dates to his letters. One would be dated, "From my hermitage," another, "From the Isle of Patmos," another, "Among the Birds," and another, "From Regions of the Air."

But the most important work that Luther did while a prisoner in Wartburg Castle, was the translation of the New Testament into the German language. Nothing that he ever did was more useful than this. Other persons had tried to do this before, but it was very imperfectly done. Luther did his work very carefully, and the translation he made was the best that had ever been made in the German language. Moses was taken up to the top of Mount Sinai, and then came down, bringing God's law, or the ten commandments, to the people. And so Luther was taken up to his resting-place in the castle on the mountain-top, and when he came down he brought to the people the "new commandment" which Jesus gave, even the gospel of life and salvation. And so the work he did in Wartburg Castle made the year he spent there the most useful year of Luther's life. No doubt some of Luther's friends thought it was a very mysterious providence which had taken him away from public work and kept him away from it so long. This is a good illustration of the way in which God "makes all things work together for good to them that love him."

Luther was not kept a close prisoner while in this castle. He had the freedom of the castle, and went hunting in the forest when he wished to do so, under the care of soldiers. He was dressed as a soldier himself, and let his hair grow long so as not to be recognized if any person should meet him. And when we see how wonderfully God took care of Luther, we should be thankful because of the great good that came to the church and to the world through his spared life. And it should also strengthen our own confidence and trust in God.

3. *His room in Wartburg Castle.* The room can still be seen in Wartburg Castle where Martin Luther, the great Reformer, had his study. The old-fashioned arm chair in which he used to sit, the square oak table on which he used to write, and hanging up over the table a sort of bookcase, with a curiously-carved front to it are all kept there now. Above the bookcase is a likeness of Luther, and round about it are several other pictures.

Even there he had trials.

4. *Luther's trials in Wartburg Castle* He left many troubles behind him when he went there, but still he carried some with him. The very best men in the world have something that is evil in their hearts.

And then Satan is sure to follow us, and tempt us by putting bad thoughts into our hearts, and this must cause us trouble. It was just so with Luther in the Wartburg Castle. He got away from the emperor and the pope, but he did not get away from Satan. This great enemy of all that is good followed him even to the quiet study in that far-off forest home. Satan came to him there, and worried him by putting bad thoughts into his mind. One day, when Luther was either dreaming, or his mind was a little wandering, he thought he saw Satan coming to him, like the "roaring lion" of which the Bible speaks. He picked up a great, heavy inkstand that was on his table, and threw it at him. The inkstand did not hit Satan, but it struck against the wall, and the ink was spilled over the plaster on the wall. The black mark on the right hand side of the wall stood there for a long time after Luther was dead, but it is not there now, for the wall has been re-plastered, and the ink spot cannot be seen. But the story is always remembered by those who go to visit Luther's study in the old Wartburg Castle.*

Luther came out of the castle in 1522, and continued his preaching, teaching and writing with greater vigor than ever. He married Catherine Von Bora, who became a great help in his work, as well as a loving companion in his home. He labored to found schools to instruct the young in the Bible, to settle disputes and troubles among the people, with great success, for he was loved as a friend by multitudes of the German folk. Luther died in 1546 at Eisleben where he was born, and whither he had gone to remove some business difficulties between laborers and their employers. So his last work was to be a peacemaker, as his life-work had been to be a faithful messenger of the Prince of Peace.

* Wartburg Castle is two or three miles east of Eisenach and was founded in 1070, and restored in its original shape in 1847. It is a long irregularly shaped pile of buildings comprising a narrow portion called the *Vorburg,* in which is Luther's room, and a broader oval shaped part called the *Hofburg* in which is the Landgraves house and apartments fitted up for a winter residence of the grand-ducal family.—E. W. R.

CHAPTER XI.

LUTHER'S MONUMENT AT WORMS.

A NOBLE monument, has been set up in the old city of Worms, to the memory of this great man, and to the memory of some others who helped him in carrying on the Reformation. No more suitable place could have been selected for this monument than the city of Worms. It was here that Luther made his celebrated defence of the Reformation, in the presence of the famous Emperor Charles V. and the great Council, called "The Diet of Worms," which the emperor had gathered together to try and make Luther give up the doctrines he was teaching. But instead of giving them up, Luther defended them manfully before all the great men there, as we have already stated. *That* was the most important thing that Luther ever did.

And so it was very proper that a monument in honor of Luther should stand in the city of Worms.*

In speaking of this monument; we will give a history of the monument, and a description of it. We begin, then, with

1. *A History of this Monument.* It would be very interesting if we could tell who was the first person who thought about this monument; and give an account of all the different steps that were taken till the work was accomplished. I cannot do this, but will go as far as I can in giving this history.

About nine years were spent in building this monument. It was begun in the year 1859, and finished in 1868. It was first uncovered for the people to look at, in the month of June in that year. They had a grand celebration on that occasion. This lasted for three days. People went from all parts of Germany to be present at the celebration. Papers were read and

* There is also a monument to Luther standing in the Market place at Wittenberg, a picture of which may be seen on page 63.—E. W. R.

speeches made about the Reformation, and the different good and great men who helped Luther to do the work. Hymns were sung, and many other things were done suitable for such a celebration.

The plan or design of the monument was made by Professor Rietschell, of the city of Berlin. The different figures represented in the monument are all in bronze. The whole cost of it was eighty-five thousand dollars. This monument will stand for ages. It shows us one of the ways in which David's words will be fulfilled when he says, "The righteous shall be had in everlasting remembrance" (Ps. 112 : 6). It also illustrates the mean- of God's own words when he says, "Them that honor me I will honor" (1 Sam. 2 : 30). And as people go from different parts of the world to look at this monument, they will feel and say, "What a glorious work the Reformation was!"

2. *A Description of this Monument.* A massive platform about fifty feet square and ten feet high has in its centre a column or pedestal surrounded by seven smaller

ones. A bronze figure of Luther stands on the centre column or pedestal. It is eleven feet high, almost twice as large as the natural size of a man. He has a Bible in his left hand. His right hand is laid upon it, and he is looking up to heaven. This was just the way in which he stood before the council, when, after making his defence, as his enemies still urged him to give up the doctrines he had taught, he uttered those famous words, "*Here I stand. I can do no otherwise. God help me. Amen!*" In front of the pedestal, and directly under where Luther stands, is an inscription. This contains the words of the great reformer just quoted above. The sides of the pedestal are ornamented with scenes from the life of Luther, and the likenesses of some of his friends. At the foot of the pedestal are four figures in a sitting posture, at the four corners. These represent four of the principal reformers in other countries, and before Luther's time, who prepared the way for his work. The old man sitting at the right hand corner of the front of the pedestal, is Wycliffe, the English Reformer. On the left hand corner the figure sitting with its right hand pointing to heaven, is Savonarola, the Italian Reformer. The figures at the back corners are Peter Waldo, and John Huss, the French and Bavarian Reformers.

Then there are four other figures in this monument for us to notice. These are the four men, standing on pedestals at the four corners of the enclosure. The figure at the right hand corner in front, represents a person standing with his sword before him. The point of it rests on the ground, and both his hands are resting on the hilt or handle of the sword. This is Philip the Generous, Landgrave of Hesse, one of the German princes who was a warm friend of Luther. The figure standing at the corner back of him, with a book in his left hand, is Melancthon, not a soldier, but a student. He was perhaps the greatest help and comfort that Luther had in all his busy life. At the left hand corner in front of the monument, is a figure holding a sword pointed up towards heaven. This is Frederic the Wise, Elector of Saxony, who protected Luther at the Diet of Worms, and had him seized on his way home and hidden away for safety in Wartburg Castle. The other figure standing back of Frederic, at the left hand corner, is John Reuchlin, a learned student, who by his writings helped on the cause of the Reformation greatly. Three female figures are seen sitting at the sides between the corner figures. These do not represent real characters, but are intended to be emblematical of the towns of Magdeburg, Augsburg, and Spires; or mourning, confession and protesting, the three great events or acts in the Reformation which took place in these towns. Between these figures are the arms of twenty-four towns in Germany which first accepted the doctrines of the Reformation.

Such is the history and description of this monument. Whenever we think of it, or the great work it commemorates, let us thank God for Luther and the Reformation!

CHAPTER XII.

PHILIP MELANCTHON. 1497–1560.

LUTHER stands out as the greatest of all the heroes of the Reformation. Like Saul, the first king of Israel, among the young men of his day, Luther rises up, head and shoulders above the other Reformers.

Philip Melancthon was the particular friend of Luther, and was a great help to him in the important work he had to do. We will speak of Melancthon *as a scholar*, *as a Christian* and *as a father*.

1. *Melancthon as a scholar*. Next to Luther, he was the most useful and important man in the great work of the Reformation. He was the second leader in this work. Melancthon was born in a little town called Bretten, in Germany, on the sixteenth of February, 1497. Luther

was born in 1483. That was fourteen years before the birth of Melancthon. And so Luther was a good stout boy fourteen years old, when his friend Melancthon was born. But as Luther was born fourteen years before Melancthon, so he died just the same number of years before his friend. They both died when they were sixty-three years old.

Melancthon was very fond of study. He was the best scholar in his class at college. He got through his studies and graduated at the University at Heidelberg, by the time he was seventeen years old. He began at once to lecture in the University of Tübingen. He soon became known as one of the most learned men of that age. When only twenty years old, he published a Greek grammar and a volume of the works of Aristotle, one of the old Greek philosophers. He could speak and write about as well in Greek as in his own native German language. He was an earnest student of the Bible all his days. And though he never was ordained or became a minister, yet he lectured on theology and wrote a great many sermons for other men to preach. He was a much more learned man than Luther, and so was able to help him in this way. And as "Moses was learned in all the wisdom of the Egyptians," to fit him for the work he had to do, in leading the Israelites out of Egypt; so Melancthon was learned in all the wisdom of his day, to make him a better help to Luther in the work of the Reformation. This was the deliverance of God's people from the church of Rome, which was a house of spiritual bondage, worse than what Egypt was to the Israelites.

2. *Melancthon as a Christian.* We have seen that Luther and Melancthon were very different men as scholars, and they were not less different as Christians. Melancthon had a great deal more learning than Luther. We do not say that he had more piety, but only that he showed it in a different way. When we become Christians we are not made exactly alike in all things. We all learn to love Jesus and try to be like him, but we show this

in different ways. You know how it is with the light of the sun when it shines through the different panes of glass in a window of stained glass. Here is a red pane, all the light which comes through that will be red. There is a blue pane, all the light that comes through that will be blue. And so with the green, and orange, and every other color. And so when the grace of God comes into our hearts and makes us Christians, it makes us Christians of different kinds, according to the difference of our natural tempers. Luther's natural temper was rough, sharp, violent. And when he became a Christian, he always had a certain roughness about him. Melancthon's natural temper was mild, and gentle, and loving; and when he became a christian, his piety was of this gentle, lamb-like kind. Luther was more like Peter or Paul among the apostles of Jesus, while Melancthon was more like the loving John. Luther was like the wind when it blows a gale and makes everything bend before it. Melancthon was like the low, soft breeze of a summer's evening, that whispers gently among the flowers. If he and Luther had both been the same, they never would have done the great work before them as they did do it. If Melancthon had been like Luther, they

The University at Wittenberg on the left; Melancthon's house towering on the right.

would have spoiled things by their hastiness and violence. And if Luther had been like Melancthon, they would neither of them have had the boldness and strength to do what *had* to be done. The church of the Reformation would have been like a body that had no backbone to it. It never could have stood up to the great work it had to do. And so God made Melancthon just such a Christian as would be the greatest help to Luther. He was like oil on the wheels of the Reformation, that made everything work smoothly.

3. *Melancthon as a father.* He married in 1420, and lived happily with his wife for thirty-seven years, till she died in 1457, three years before his own death. He was very fond of his home and his children. He used to call his nursery "*the little church.*" And sometimes when visitors would call to see Philip Melancthon, they would find this great man, this learned professor, who was known as "*the teacher of Germany,*" with his student's gown on sitting in the nursery, holding in one hand a book, which he was reading, while with the other hand *he was rocking the cradle!* Whatever we do for God, let us try, like Melancthon, to "do it with our might."

W Tindale.

CHAPTER XIII.

WILLIAM TYNDALE. 1484–1536.

Having spoken of Luther and Melancthon, and the Reformation in Germany, we will now take a look at what was going on about the same time in England.

On another page we have a portrait of Tyndale, one of the English "Heroes of the Reformation." He was born at Hunt's court, North Nibley, in Gloucestershire, England, in the year 1484—over four hundred years ago, and the next year after the birth of the great Reformer, Martin Luther. The family of Tyndale is an ancient one, and was settled for centuries on the banks of the Tyne in Northumberland. One of the stock was a baron, owning Langley Castle. In the wars between the houses of York and Lancaster, the then baron lost his property and title, and fled to Gloucestershire. There are several ways of spelling Tyndale's name. Sometimes it is spelled Tindal, Tyndal, Tindale, or Tyndale, as it is at the head of this chapter, William Tyndale. He went through college at Oxford, and graduated there. Then he went to Cambridge, the other great university town in England, and there it is said that he studied and took another degree. He was very industrious in his studies, and had a great love for the scriptures.

In the year 1502 he was ordained to the ministry, when he was only eighteen years old. He then became a priest to the nunnery of Lambley, in Carlisle.

Even then many persons were beginning to feel that there ought to be a change in some of the corrupt practices of the church of Rome, and Tyndale shared in those feelings. He had been a diligent student of the New Testament in the Greek language while he was in college, and it was thus that he learned to know and love "the truth as it in Jesus."

And when he felt how important the

knowledge of this truth was to the salvation and comfort of his own soul, this feeling kindled in his heart the desire to bring this truth within the reach of others. He tried to scatter the light that God gave him. He did this by talking about the Bible; by preaching about it; and by translating it into the language of the people. One day a priest with whom he was arguing, said: "It was better to be without God's law than the pope's." This provoked him very much, and he said: "If God spare my life, I will make it so in England, that the ploughboys will know more of the Bible than many of the priests now do." And this came to pass.

Then he became a tutor in the family of an English nobleman near Bristol. While occupied in teaching during the week, he used to spend his Sundays in preaching all round that neighborhood. He had controversies with the Romish priests about their false doctrines. This occasioned him considerable trouble. Then he concluded to go up to London, and try to find employment there.

All this time his mind was full of the idea of translating the New Testament into English; but he soon found, as he himself said, "that there was no room in the palace of the Lord Bishop of London for translating the New Testament. He however lived for a time with an alderman, and was privately busy in his work of translating the New Testament. The alderman was soon suspected of heresy and sent to the tower.

So Tyndale left England and went to Hamburg, in Germany. From there he went to Cologne. For he wished to print his Bible. Now in the days of Wycliffe, of whom we spoke in a former chapter, the art of printing was not known, but before the time came for the Reformation, the printing press had been invented. Without this, the great work of the Reformation never could have been carried on. It would have been impossible to multiply copies of the Bible fast enough to meet the wants of the people. With a written Bible very little could have been done; but with a *printed* Bible, great things could be done. At Cologne, it is supposed Tyndale began to print his New Testament in English. But finding some unexpected difficulty in his way, he went to the city of Worms, on the Rhine; and here the first two editions of the New Testament in English were published. The copies of the scriptures which Tyndale had made were sent over to England by trusty friends, and secretly scattered freely there. How they were received by the Romish prelates we shall see in another chapter. It was probably about this time that Tyndale met his fellow-reformers in Germany.

CHAPTER XIV.

BUYING TYNDALE'S BIBLES. 1526.

THE king of England at this time was a Romanist. He was not willing to allow the Bible to be printed in his country. But on the continent Tyndale, by the help of some friends in England, printed an edition of fifteen hundred copies of the New Testament. These were sent over to England. Some of them were sold, and some were given away. People in different parts of the country could now for the first time, have the Bible in their homes, and so were able to read, "in their own tongue the wonderful works of God."*

* The following is a specimen of Tyndale's translation. It is the account of the healing of the cripple at the pool of Bethesda, John 5 : 2. This will permit our young readers to compare it with Wycliffe's version of the same miracle, given on p. 29, and to notice the progress in the English tongue which had taken place in two centuries.

Sale of Tyndale's Bibles.

The bald-headed man on the left side of the picture, with his arm resting on the pile of books, represents Tyndale. The books on which he is leaning are copies of the Bible which he had translated. The other person in the picture, emptying money from his purse upon the table, is Packington, who came to Tyndale to buy up all the Bibles he had to sell.

Soon after Tyndale's New Testament was published, and it began to be circulated in England, a law was passed forbidding any persons to buy or read

"There is at Jerusalem, by the slaughterhousse a pole called in the ebrue tonge, bethesda, havynge five porches, in them laye a greate multitude off sicke folke, off blynde, halt, and wyddered, waytynge for the movynge off the wather. For an angell went doune at a certayne ceason into the pole an stered the water. whosoever then fyrst after the sterynge oft the water stepped doune was made whoale of whatsoever disease he had. And a certayne man was there, which had bene diseased xxxviij. yeares. When Jesus sawe hym lye, and knewe that he nowe longe tyme had bene diseased, he sayde vnto hym: Wilt thou be whoale? The syke answered hym: Syr, I have no man when the water is moved, to put me into the pole. Butt in the meane tyme, whill I am about to come, another stoppeth doune before me.

"Jesus sayde vnto hym, ryse, take vp thy beed and walke. And immediatly that man was whole, and toke vp his beed, and went. And the same daye was the saboth daye."

the book. But instead of stopping persons from doing this, the passage of that law only made them more eager than ever to get the book. The bishop of London at that time was a very violent Romanist. He hated the Bible greatly, and tried hard to stop the circulation of it. He thought the best way to do this would be to buy up all the copies of the scriptures he could find and burn them. So he employed Mr. Packington, a merchant who knew Tyndale, to buy from him all the copies of the New Testament he had to sell. The bishop had plenty of money, so he told his agent not to mind about the price. The bargain was made. The Bibles were bought. This is represented in the picture on another page. They were carried over to London, and the bishop had a great bonfire made of them near St. Paul's cross. He thought he had stopped the circulation of the scriptures. But it was not so. For Tyndale took the money he had received for the Bibles, and printed a larger and better edition than before. And soon the bishop found that instead of stopping the circulation of the scriptures, he had only increased it; for in the place of every Bible he had burned, ever so many more made their appearance. Though it was forbidden to bring the Bible over openly into England, they continued to be brought in large numbers, hidden away in cargoes of wheat or in bundles of merchandise, which vessels brought from the continent.

One man in London, very zealous in selling the scriptures, was taken up and brought to trial. During the trial the judge asked him if he knew who it was who was helping Tyndale print so many Bibles. His reply was that the bishop of London was doing more to help him than any one else, for the money paid for the Bibles that were burned had been used in printing and circulating fresh copies.

1. *How easy it is to make a mistake.* The bishop of London thought he had hit upon an excellent plan to stop the circulation of the scriptures, but he made a mistake. He "outwitted himself" as the old proverb runs. His plan worked exactly the other

way. He might as well have tried to put out a fire on the hearth by pouring oil upon it. The Bible tells us how God "taketh the wise"—those who think themselves so—"in their own craftiness" (Job 5:13). And David tells us how wicked people sometimes dig a pit, and fall into it themselves (Ps. 9:15). We see both these passages illustrated in the mistake which the bishop of London made. How easy it is to make mistakes!

2. *How easily God can bring good out of evil.* If you and I had been present at the bonfire of the Bibles, which this bishop made in London, when we saw cart-loads of that blessed book brought out and flung into the flames, we should have thought that a sad day for the cause of the Bible. But if we could have gone from there directly over to see Tyndale setting the printing-press to work, and sending out ten Bibles for every one the bishop had burned, we should have felt very differently about it. And this is the way in which God is working all the time. He is bringing good out of what seems to

be evil. The Bible is full of illustrations of this truth. We see it in the history of Joseph, and of Moses, and of Job, and of David. And we see the same thing all around us.

3. *It is a poor business to work against God.* The bishop of London was working against God when he tried to stop the Bible from being circulated. He might as well have tried to stop the sun from shining, or the wind from blowing, or the tide from coming in. He found at last that it *was* a poor business. Pharaoh, king of Egypt, was working against God when he resolved not to let the Israelites go. But when at last he and his army were overwhelmed in the waters of the Red Sea, he found that it was a poor business. To work *with* God and *for* God is a good business; *it pays.* But to work *against* God is a poor business; *it does not pay.*

4. *Tyndale in prison.* Perhaps you will ask how so good a man came to be in prison? The enemies of the Bible wanted to stop his work of printing Bibles. So

they got authority from the pope to have him arrested. They engaged a secret emissary of the king of England, but who pretended to be a friend to visit Brussels, and find out where Tyndale was, and lay plans for taking him a prisoner. He was betrayed, arrested, and thrown into prison and kept there for eighteen months. While in prison at Vilvoorden, the priests often came to argue with him and try to get him back to the church of Rome. Three priests are there, and Tyndale is standing up with his hand on the open Bible, proving by its blessed words the truth of what he taught. Finding they could not convert him, sentence of death was pronounced against him. He was bound to the stake, strangled by a rope drawn round his neck, and then his body was burned to ashes. This took place in the year 1536, in the fifty-second year of his age. His last words were this prayer: "O Lord, open the king of England's eyes." There is no telling how much good he did, in helping on the great work of the Reformation, by translating into

English and scattering abroad the word of life so freely.

Two lessons may be learned from the life of this distinguished Reformer.

1. *A lesson of industry.* It was the patient, persevering industry with which he pursued his studies while at college, till he had gained so complete a mastery of the Greek language, which led to all the great usefulness of his after life; and industry in school or in college is the path leading to success in the business of life. Tell me how a boy or youth behaves in school or in college, and I will tell what sort of man he is likely to make.

When the great Duke of Wellington was talking with a friend one day about the famous battle of Waterloo, in which he defeated Napoleon Bonaparte, he said, "The victory of Waterloo was gained at Eton." That was the name of the college to which the duke went when he was a young man; and what he meant by this saying was that the habits of industry and perseverance which he, and some of his officers, formed while students at Eton

College had led to their success in life, including this victory at Waterloo.

And this is true of all young persons. Tyndale's success in helping on the great work of the Reformation was, with God's blessing, owing to the habit of industry which he formed in college.

2. *The power of prayer.* Just before his death, when Tyndale was fastened to the stake, he lifted up his eyes to heaven, and offered this prayer: "Lord, open the eyes of England's king." Henry VIII. was king of England then. He had opposed in every way the circulation of the scriptures through his kingdom; but the prayer of the dying martyr was heard. The king's eyes were opened; and very soon after this he made a law placing a copy of the Word of God in every church in England, so that all the people might there read it or hear it read; and within a year after Tyndale's death seven or eight editions of the New Testament were circulated through England by royal permission, and appointed to be placed in the churches for the use of the people.

Let us all have strong faith in the power of prayer, and let us use it more constantly, in connection with everything that we attempt to do, for the glory of God, for the good of others, or for our own good.

CHAPTER XV.

EDWARD THE SIXTH. 1547–1553.

In speaking of the good men who helped on the blessed work of the Reformation in England, we must not forget Edward the Sixth, the young king who succeeded Henry VIII. He was one of the most interesting characters connected with this work. Our Saviour said to Peter when he was on earth, "What I do, thou knowest not now, but thou shalt know hereafter." There are many things to which these words apply. And the early death of this good young king is one of them. We cannot understand now why he was permitted to die so soon, but when we get to heaven we shall know all about it.

There are *three* things about this good young king of which we will speak.

Edward the Sixth and the Bible.

1. *King Edward's early piety.* He was the son of the famous king Henry the Eighth, and was born in the year 1537. His mother died very soon after his birth. His father was very careful about his education, and when he was only six years old, he selected two very excellent men, one a pious nobleman and the other a faithful minister of the gospel, to be his teachers. Those good men did everything they could for his improvement. And they found him very willing to learn, and very ready to profit by their help. He made such progress in his studies, that before he was nine years of age he could write very well. Several letters and compositions written by him at this time, in Latin and French, have been saved, and are kept as curiosities in the British Museum.

The good Archbishop Cranmer was also one of the instructors of the young prince. So we see that he had every advantage possible for him to have. But better than all, the Lord himself was his teacher, and "who teacheth like him?" It was he who called Samuel when a child, to be his servant. And it was this same gracious God who called this young prince to know and serve him, when he was not older than Samuel. And like Samuel, he heard God's call and obeyed it. May all young friends who read this be called in the same way, and like Samuel and the young Prince Edward, may they obey the call!

2. *King Edward's love for the Bible.* He showed this love in several ways. One of these was by diligently reading it. Another was by his desire to understand it as well as read it. But best of all, he showed his love of the Bible by trying to carry out its teachings, and to live in the way in which it tells us to live.

Two interesting incidents are mentioned of young Edward, which show how great his love and reverence for the Bible were. One of these is illustrated by the picture on another page. The young prince was in the library one day. He wished to get something from an upper shelf, which was beyond his reach. A large book was lying on the table. One of his attendants took it up and laid it on the floor for him to stand on. Edward saw it was the Bible. Lifting it from the floor he placed it reverently on the table again, and then laying his hand on it, said very earnestly, "This is God's blessed book. It is not right that we should trample under our feet that which he has given us to treasure up in our heads and hearts."

The other incident is connected with his coronation, or the act of making him king. In countries where they have kings this is always a great occasion. Edward's father died when he was only ten years old. At that tender age he was made king. A great procession was formed on that occasion. Three swords were brought in to be carried before him in that procession. These represented his three kingdoms, England, Ireland and Scotland. Edward said another sword was wanted, which was the Bible or the sword of the Spirit. And he insisted on having a Bible carried with those three swords, to show that it was from the Word of God that he derived his authority as king.

3. *The good King Edward died.* He reigned only six years. He died in his sixteenth year from an attack of small-pox. But in that short time he did a great deal of good. He had the scriptures circulated all through the country. Thirty-six different editions of the whole Bible or of the New Testament, were printed and sold during his reign. Besides these, portions of the Bible and other good books in great numbers were spread abroad everywhere. The images were removed from the churches, and the laws known as the "Bloody statutes" were repealed. And then he established and gave money to support hospitals for the sick and schools for the poor, which continue to this day, and for the last three hundred years have been the means of doing great good to hundreds and thousands of people.

Let us try to follow the example of this young king, by loving God, by loving his Word, and by doing all the good we can.

John Fox.

CHAPTER XVI.

JOHN FOX. 1517–1587.

AMONG the good and great men whose lives we are now considering there were few more useful than John Fox. His name is very often written Foxe. He was buried in the famous old church of St. Giles, Cripplegate, London. In the chancel wall of this church is a marble slab containing a Latin inscription, which put into English gives an account of his life and labors, as in the copy of it on the next page.

Not far from his grave lie the remains of Milton, the celebrated poet, who wrote the well known poem of Paradise Lost.

In speaking of John Fox we will refer to *the facts of his life, and the lessons which they teach us.*

The facts of his life are these: he was

born at Boston, Lincolnshire, England, in the year 1517, the same year in which Luther began the work of the Reformation in Germany. He was educated at Braz-

To JOHN FOX,
The most faithful Martyrologist of the Church of England.
The most Sagacious Investigator of Historical Antiquity.
The most valiant Defender of Evangelical Truth,
A wondrous Worker of Miracles.
Who presented the Mariam Martyrs, like phœnixes, alive from their ashes.
Chiefly to fulfill every duty of filial affection,
Samuel Fox,
His Eldest Son,
Erected this monument,
Not without tears.
He died the 18th of April, A. D. 1587,
A Septuagenarian.

enose College, or King's Hall, Oxford, where he attained great distinction for his earnestness and success as a student. He received the degree of A.B. in 1538, and was elected Fellow of Magdalen College in 1543. While he was a student in college he was a thorough Romanist; but soon after he had graduated, he learned to know "the truth as it is in Jesus," and then became an earnest and devoted Protestant. In the year 1545 he was accused of heresy, and as he boldly proclaimed his opinions in favor of the Protestant Reformation, he was expelled from his college. Then for several years he supported himself by acting as private tutor, first in the family of Sir Thomas Lucy of Warwickshire and afterwards in the household of the Duke of Norfolk.

When the persecution against the Protestants was raging under the reign of Queen Mary, he found that his life was in danger, and leaving England he went over to the continent. He made his home then at Basle, in Switzerland. It was while residing there that he began to write his great life-work, "The Acts and Monuments of the Church, or the Book of Martyrs." Many editions of this work have been published, of various sizes, and no one can tell how much good it did by spreading abroad and supporting Protestant truth in

England. The first edition was issued in 1563.

After the death of Mary, when her sister Elizabeth became queen of England, persecution ceased, and the cause of Protestantism revived and prospered. Then Fox returned to England. His former pupil the Duke of Norfolk gave him a pension for his support. He was also appointed prebendary, or occasional preacher, in the cathedral of Salisbury. And thus he spent the rest of his days greatly esteemed by all who knew him, for his profound learning, his deep humility, his earnest piety; and amidst the blessings of the nation, he died in 1587, when he had just reached the 70th year of his age. Such are the principal facts of this good man's life.

And now let us look at *the lessons* taught us by these facts.

1. *The lesson of diligence.* He entered college in the 16th year of his age, and was noted for the diligence with which he pursued his studies. Of course he was successful, for this is the result to which

diligence always leads. As a proof of his diligence in study, we are told that before he was 30 years of age, or in less than 12 years from the time he first entered college, he had read all the Greek and Latin fathers, all the writings of the schoolmen, and all the acts of the different councils of the church, besides making himself master of the Hebrew language. And this same diligence was practiced by him in all his life work.

Many years ago a little boy entered the famous school at Harrow, in England. He was put into a class for which he was not ready. The other boys had studied books which he knew nothing about. Of course he was at the tail of the class. The teacher scolded him and the boys made fun of him; but he resolved to try what he could do. He got the books the other boys had studied and resolved to master them. The hours of play and many of the hours of sleep he gave up to diligent study. Soon he rose in his class. He got to the head of it, and kept his place there. He became the pride of the

Harrow school. And to-day, if you and I should visit St. Paul's Cathedral in London, we should see a beautiful marble statue of the greatest Oriental scholar England has ever known. His name is Sir William Jones.

2. *The lesson of perseverance.* Whatever Fox undertook to do, he not only did with diligence, but he *kept on doing it* till it was accomplished. The great work of his life was the history of the martyrs. This work was made up of eight volumes. It began with an account of the martyrs of the tenth century, and then went on with their history for the next five centuries. In writing this work he was constantly occupied in untiring labor for eleven long years. In his anxiety to have every statement in his work correct and truthful, he examined all the records of the martyrs over and over again with the most persevering diligence; and the result of this is, that the history of the martyrs which he wrote is a work that is most thoroughly reliable. And when we think of the untiring perseverance which this noble hero

of the Reformation displayed in finishing his great work, we have a lesson set before us which we should all try to imitate. No matter what our learning or ability may be, we shall never be able to accomplish much unless we learn and practice this lesson of perseverance.

3. *The lesson of practical usefulness.* He was not content with the constant preaching of the gospel, nor with the amount of time and labor bestowed on the great work with which his name is connected. His constant aim was to be doing good to those about him. He was remarkable for his sympathy with the poor, and for his liberality in ministering to their wants. It is said that a friend once inquired of him whether he remembered a poor man whom he used to relieve. His answer was, "Yes, I remember him very well. I am willing to forget lords and ladies, but I cannot forget such as he." He was remarkable for his kindness in comforting persons who were in sorrow and trouble. It is said that his home was constantly frequented by persons of all

ranks, from the nobility down to the poorest in the neighborhood. They would come to him for advice and consolation, and he never failed to lead them to the God that comforteth those that are cast down. And in pursuing such a course he was truly following the example of our great Master, "who went about doing good." Let us all try to imitate the example of this good man, and to practice the lessons of *diligence*, of *perseverance*, and of *practical usefulness*, so well illustrated in his life.

CHAPTER XVII.

LATIMER, 1491–1555, AND RIDLEY, 1500–1555.

DURING the terrible persecution in the reign of Queen Mary, some of the most touching and impressive incidents in the history of the Reformation in England, took place. Two noted and venerable men were chained to a stake and burned to death for trying to preach the gospel. This solemn event took place on the 15th of October, 1555, in the reign of Queen Mary. The names of these good men were Latimer and Ridley. They were both bishops in the church of England. Bishop Latimer was sixty-four years old at the time of his martyrdom; and Bishop Ridley was fifty-five. As they walked to the stake, Ridley, the younger of the two martyrs, said to his friend, "Be of good heart, brother; God will either assuage the fury of the flame, or else strengthen us to bear it." And as they were being bound to the stake, Latimer said to his companion, "Be of good comfort, master Ridley, and play the man. We shall this day light such a candle, by God's grace, in England, as I trust shall never be put out." They are usually mentioned together, because they were condemned and burnt as martyrs at the same time and place.

Let us look at the life of Latimer. Bishop Latimer was born in the year 1491, near Leicester, England. He was educated at Cambridge. When his education was finished, he became a Greek professor in the college; then he was ordained a priest. At first he was a zealous Romanist, and then he became an earnest Protestant. He was appointed rector of the church at West Kingston in 1531; was made bishop of Worcester in 1535; resigned this office in 1539, and then passed through many changes and trials till the time of his martyrdom. In Bishop Latimer's character, there are three things in which we shall find him a model most worthy of our imitation.

1. *He was a model of decision.* It is very important for us all to form this habit when we are young. Our success, both in the business of life and in the service of God, will depend greatly on it. Latimer had been brought up in all the errors of the church of Rome. He knew little of the Bible; he thought that the Romish church was right in all its teachings. He hated Luther and the Reformers and the doctrines they taught. He was all the time warning the people not to listen to any of their teachings. But he had a friend in the ministry whose name was Bilney; he had become a Protestant, and a very earnest preacher of the doctrines of the Reformation.

On one occasion Bilney came to spend an evening with his friend Latimer in his study. He brought his New Testament with him, and read it to him, telling him about the way of salvation in Christ Jesus. He talked affectionately to him, and prayed earnestly with him. That evening's visit from his friend Bilney led to Latimer's conversion. As soon as he saw the light of God's truth shining clearly before him, he made up his mind at once to follow it. He decided to give up the errors of Rome and become a Protestant. He acted with decision in the matter.

2. *Bishop Latimer stands before us as a model of faithfulness.* From the time when his eyes were opened to see and understand the gospel of Jesus, he was untiring in his efforts to make it known to others. While rector of the church at West Kingston, and bishop of Worcester, it might well have been said of him that, like the apostle Paul, he had determined to know nothing else among men, save Jesus Christ and him crucified. He was an earnest, eloquent preacher. It was something new in those days to have such preaching, and great numbers of people followed him wherever he went, hungering for the truth in Jesus, as he preached it.

3. *Latimer was a model of courage.* Wherever the path of duty opened before

him he went boldly forward and did what he felt was right, without a moment's hesitation. The Romish priests united together and tried to stop him from preaching the doctrines of the Reformation: but he was not afraid of them. He went boldly on and did the work which he felt sure that God had sent him to do. Then the bishops tried to stop him. They advised him not to put the Bible in the hands of the people. But he felt that he must do it; and he did it. They threatened him with a trial and imprisonment. He did not mind their threats, but went on bravely with his work. No doubt they would have put him in prison only Henry VIII. king of England was his friend, and gave him liberty to go on preaching the gospel, as he believed it right to do.

This brave man showed his courage in the most striking way, when he was made chaplain to the king, and appointed to preach before him. The other chaplains were very careful to avoid saying anything before the king which they thought he would not like. But Latimer acted differently. While speaking before the king of England, he never forgot that he was also speaking before the King of heaven, and his first desire always was to say what he knew would be pleasing to the Lord. This gave him courage to say some things before the king which no one else ever dared to say. But yet the king had such confidence in him that he never was offended at anything this brave, honest man felt called upon to say.

And then just before his death this good man showed his courage in a very striking way. Henry VIII. and his son Edward VI. had died. Then Mary, the daughter of Henry, was made queen. She was a bigoted Romanist. As soon as she ascended the throne she began to persecute the Protestants. So many good people were put to death by her orders that she was called "Bloody Mary." She sent a messenger to summon Bishop Latimer to London, having made up her mind that he should be burnt at the stake. Latimer heard of this a good while before the messenger arrived. He had time enough to have gone away, and so have escaped the painful death that was awaiting him. Some of his friends advised him to do so. But he would not take their advice. With the heroic courage that belonged to him, he preferred to seal with his blood the great truths of the gospel which he had spent his life in preaching. And this courage brought him to the stake.

Let us remember these three model points in the character of this good martyr, and let us try to follow his example of *decision*, of *faithfulness*, and of *courage*. And if we do this, it will with God's blessing make us good and useful.

CHAPTER XVIII.

THOMAS CRANMER. 1489–1556.

THERE was perhaps no one who did more to help on the great work of the Reformation in England than this good man who suffered martyrdom in 1556. In speaking about Archbishop Cranmer, there are *four* things of which I wish to say something. These are: *his character, his work, his fall, and his death.*

1. *His character.* Thomas Cranmer was born in July, 1489, in the town of Aslacton, in Nottinghamshire, England. His father was a respectable gentleman. Cranmer was sent to college at Cambridge. After graduating he remained there some years, studying diligently different branches of learning. It was in this way, as well as by the earnest study of the Bible, that he fitted himself for the positions of great

Cranmer at the Stake.

usefulness which he afterwards filled. After his ordination as priest, he rose from one position to another, till King Henry VIII. became acquainted with him. He was so pleased with his learning and piety that he had him appointed Archbishop of Canterbury. This is the highest position in the church of England, and one in which a good man can do a great deal of good. And Archbishop Cranmer was a good man. No doubt he had his faults, as we all have. But he was not only very learned, but very humble, and pious, and kind, and gentle.

There is no harder lesson for us to learn as Christians than that of returning good for evil. But Cranmer had learned this lesson so well, that they used to say, "If you want to make the Archbishop your friend, the surest way is to do him some injury." I am afraid there are not many Christians of whom this could be said. This is certainly a lovely character which this good man gained for himself.

2. *His work for the Reformation.* There are several things about this work to look

at. One of these was *the separation of the church of England from the church of Rome.* Henry VIII. had a quarrel with the pope about his wives. No doubt many wrong things were done by the king in this matter, but God overruled them all for good. If it had not been for this quarrel, the Reformation in England might not have taken place at all, or might not have been so successful. But the learning and wisdom of Cranmer were useful in bringing the king's quarrel to such an end that England was separated from Rome. This was one way in which the Reformation in England was helped on by Cranmer.

Another way in which he did this was *by printing and circulating the scriptures.* He had a new and revised edition of the Bible printed under his own eye. Copies of this blessed book were placed in the principal churches, and chained to the reading desk. The churches were open at all times, so that any of the people who wished to do so could go in whenever they wanted to read God's word for themselves.

Another way in which Cranmer helped on the Reformation was *by the changes which he made in the church of England.* The prayers that had been in Latin were translated into English. The altars were changed into communion tables. The use of incense and candles in day-time, and many such practices were stopped. If you go into a Romish church to-day, and then into an evangelical Episcopal church, and notice the difference in their services, you will get a good idea of what Cranmer did for the church of England, in helping to make its worship evangelical and Protestant. And then as very few of the ministers of that day were able to prepare sermons of their own, he had a volume of sermons, or "homilies," as they were called, printed, and the ministers were ordered to read them in the churches. And in this way the people were taught the nature of true religion, as they would not otherwise have been.

3. *The fall of Cranmer.* He continued his good work for the Reformation during the reign of Henry VIII. and his pious

and promising young son, Edward VI. But Edward died, and his sister Mary was made queen. Mary was a Romanist. During her reign the work of the Reformation stood still, and everything was changed. Cranmer was turned out of his office and thrown into prison. Protestants were required to change their religion. Many who would not do this were imprisoned or put to death. Cranmer was called upon to give up his Protestant faith and profess himself a Romanist. He refused to do it. Then he was threatened with death by burning unless he changed his religion, while the promise of life and honor was held out to him if he made this change. He was now a feeble old man. His enemies worked upon his fears, and in a moment of weakness he signed a paper stating that he had given up his Protestantism and become a Romanist. This was his sad fall. But we must not blame him too much. Can we be sure that we should have done any better if we had been in his situation? Cranmer recovered from his fall, and died a true martyr.

4. *The death of Cranmer.* He had no sooner committed this sin of saying he would give up his religion, than he repented of it. His cruel enemies resolved to put him to death in spite of his professed change. They expected that he would die confirming at the stake what he had written in prison, but in this they were disappointed. Before his death he made an address to the people. At the close of it he used these words: "And now I come to the great thing that troubles my conscience, more than any other thing I ever did in my life, and that is the setting abroad of writings contrary to the truths which I thought in my heart, for fear of death and to save my life, if it might be; and all such things which I have written or signed with my own hand since my degradation I now proclaim untrue. And forasmuch as my hand offended, in writing contrary to my heart, therefore my hand shall first be punished, for if I may come to the fire, it shall be first burned. And as for the pope, I refuse him as Christ's enemy, and anti-Christ

with all his false doctrines." This filled his enemies with astonishment and rage. They hurried him to the stake. Dressed in a long robe, that reached from his neck to his ankles, he was chained to the stake. His feet were bare, his head was bald, and his beard long and white. As the flames rose around him, he moved no more than the stake to which he was bound. His eyes were lifted up to heaven, and stretching forth his hand into the flame, he exclaimed, "This hand hath offended; oh, this unworthy right hand!" And then, using the words of the first martyr, Stephen, "Lord Jesus, receive my spirit," in the greatness of the flame he gave up the ghost. So died the good Archbishop Cranmer.

Preaching at St. Paul's Cross, London.

CHAPTER XIX.

ST. PAUL'S CROSS, LONDON.

St. Paul's Cross is a very interesting spot in the history of the Reformation. Let us state three things concerning it.

1. *What was St. Paul's Cross?* In the Romish church, before the Reformation, they got into the habit of using painted crosses, and wooden crosses, and stone crosses, in their churches and other places. If a person on a journey was saved from some great danger, he would set up a cross in memory of his preservation. When the funeral procession of a great person took place, the points along the road where the procession halted, either for resting or for some service, would afterwards be marked by a cross.

In the year 1290 A. D., when Eleanor, a famous queen of England, died, she was buried in Westminster Abbey, in London. In going there her funeral procession halted at fifteen different places. A cross was afterwards set up at each of these places. Several of these became famous places. St. Paul's Cross, was one of these. In place of the simple cross first set up here, a large, substantial stone pulpit was afterwards built. It had a platform in front, with a cupola back of it, on the top of which was a cross. You see a monk in the pulpit preaching. Some other monks are near him, and a crowd of people in front of him. And so, in answer to the question *what St. Paul's Cross was*, it is enough to say it was a famous preaching place!

2. *Where was St. Paul's Cross?* It was in the churchyard connected with St. Paul's Cathedral in London. This is a very large building, with a high dome. It can be seen from all parts of London, and every one who has visited this famous city remembers St. Paul's Cathedral. It was built two hundred years ago, by the celebrated architect Sir Christopher Wren.

Thirty-five years were occupied in finishing this building. But for centuries before the erection of the present building there had been a church on this spot. The region where it stands is now, and has been for a long time, one of the busiest parts of London. The streets around it are narrow and crowded. Any one who has ever been in Paternoster Row, near this cathedral, will never forget it. If you and I were going through this narrow, crowded street to-day, in the very heart of London, we could hardly believe that in the thirteenth century naughty boys stole apples from the orchards which were growing there, where Paternoster Row stands now. Yet it was so. And there, in the yard of this old church, in the midst of a large grass-plot, stood the famous "St. Paul's Cross."

3. *What was the history of St. Paul's Cross?* This history is very interesting. When this cross was first set up, it was only used as a place for prayer. The Romish church taught then, and still teaches, the doctrine of praying for the

dead. And as St. Paul's Cross first stood in the graveyard connected with St. Paul's Church, the first use made of it was to remind people in passing by to stop a moment and pray for the dead who were buried in the graveyard. Now we, as Protestants, do not believe in praying for the dead. We do not think it right to do so. But most men thought differently then. And long after St. Paul's Cross was first set up, if you and I had been standing there, we should have seen men and women stop by that cross, and kneel down and pray for the souls of the dead buried in that churchyard.

Another use made of St. Paul's Cross was as *a place for burning Bibles.* In the early days of the Reformation, when the Bible was first printed and circulated, the priests and bishops of the Romish church tried with all their power to stop the circulation of the Bible. When they found a Bible or Testament among any of their people they took it from them. They bought up all the copies of the scriptures they could find. And when they had collected a great pile of them, they used to have a large gathering of the people at St. Paul's Cross. Then a bonfire would be made, and all the Bibles found would be burned in the presence of the people assembled there.

After this St. Paul's Cross was used for another and a better purpose. The best preachers of the Reformation went there to preach the Gospel. Crowds of poor people would gather in front of the cross, and stand or sit on rough benches in the open air, and listen to the precious truths of the gospel. The rich would often come in their carriages or on horseback, and get near enough to hear the gospel. And then along the side of the church there were covered places, with comfortable seats in them, where persons belonging to the nobility of England would come and listen to the words of life.

If you and I should visit London now, and should try to find St. Paul's Cross, we should be disappointed. It is no longer there. It was destroyed more than two hundred years ago. But if we should go to No. 65 St. Paul's Churchyard,—this is the name of a street near the church,—we should find a large building there. This is the Depository of the Religious Tract Society, which was organized in 1799, and has distributed millions of pages of good books and tracts. It stands on the very spot once occupied by St. Paul's Cross. And just there where the enemies of the Bible once tried to stop it from being circulated, the friends of the Bible are now using the printing press to scatter its precious truths all over the world.

John Knox's House.

CHAPTER XX.

JOHN KNOX. 1505–1572.

No account of the great work of the Reformation would be complete or full that did not have something to say about that very remarkable man, John Knox. He fearlessly preached the reformed doctrines before Mary, Queen of Scots.

In speaking of Knox there are three things that we may consider: his life, his work, and his character.

1. *The life of Knox.* He was born in the year 1505. This was over three hundred and eighty years ago. It was about twenty-two years after the birth of Martin Luther, the greatest of all the Reformers. He was born at a place called Gifford Gate, near Haddington, Scotland. In that neighborhood there is a small field which is still call· d "Knox's Croft." Croft

means a small piece of land and so Knox's croft means the field or land on which Knox was born. He tells us that his father and grandfather did service under the celebrated Earl of Bothwell. He received his early education at the grammar school at Haddington, near where he was born, and finished it at the University of St. Andrews, at Glasgow. In college he was remarkable for the great power he had as a debater and speaker. The wonderful ability he afterwards had as a preacher was showing itself in him then.

He was ordained a priest in the Romish church about the year 1530, when he was twenty-five years old. It sounds strange to speak of John Knox as a Romish priest. But we must remember that before the Reformation, the church of Rome was the only so-called Christian church in the world.

For some years after this we have no particular account of what he was doing. In 1543, thirteen years after his ordination, he openly professed himself a Protestant. He had probably been studying the Bible and the early fathers of the church. This convinced him of the errors of the Romish church, and led him to join the Reformers. Then he was deposed from the priesthood, and had to share in the persecutions which the Reformers received from the Romanists. With some of his countrymen he was taken prisoner by the French. They carried him over into their country, and for nearly two years he was compelled to do hard work as a galley slave. A galley was a low, flat, one-decked vessel, much used in the Mediterranean Sea in those days, and which was chiefly moved by long, heavy oars. The men who worked these oars were chained to their seats. They had hard work and poor fare.

Knox bore this patiently, for his love to the cause of that Saviour whom he served. When released from this imprisonment he returned to his labors in behalf of the Reformation. He was found sometimes in England, sometimes on the Continent, with Calvin and other good men; but mostly in his own loved Scotland did he spend his days, amidst many dangers and difficulties, laboring earnestly to make the precious gospel of Jesus known to his countrymen.

Thus he continued till the year 1572, when he died, worn out with hard work, in the sixty-seventh year of his age. Such was the life of this great man.

2. *The work of Knox.* The great work to which John Knox gave his life was the Reformation of the church in Scotland. When the errors of the Romish church were driven away, when the power of that church over the people was destroyed and the Presbyterian church was established in its stead, that was the greatest blessing ever bestowed on the country of Scotland. And in securing this great blessing to that land, the chief agency which God employed was John Knox.

In carrying on this work, one of the greatest difficulties that Knox met with was found in the influence of Mary, Queen of Scots. She was the daughter of James V., king of Scotland, but was connected through her mother with the king of France. She was a very beautiful and very able, but a very bad woman. She was born and brought up in the Romish church, and tried all in her power to have that church preserved in Scotland with all its errors and all its wickedness. This gave Knox a great deal of trouble. He had more difficulty in managing this one bad woman than any other person. She sometimes sent for him, that she might see and hear him. He talked to her, explained the Bible and preached to her. What he said had great power with her. It often moved her to tears, but it did not make her a Protestant; and if Mary was a trouble to Knox, he was no less a trouble to her. He stood in the way of her plans. She could generally make those about her do just what she wanted to have done. But it was not so with Knox; she managed others, but she could not manage him. He was just as unmoved by all she did and said as the solid rock is unmoved by the waters of the sea that dash themselves upon it. Mary used to say "that she was more afraid of John Knox and his prayers than of an army of men." And so, in spite of the queen and the priests and the pope, John Knox, by the help of God, succeeded in breaking up the Romish church in Scotland, and establishing the Presbyterian church in its place.

And then Knox was a great help to the English Reformers in getting rid of popery, and establishing a Protestant church in their country. He spent a good deal of time in England, preaching the gospel there. They even offered to make him a bishop; but he declined the offer, because he liked the government and worship of the Presbyterian church better than that of the church of England.

To be the chief means of establishing a Protestant church in Scotland, and to help in establishing a Protestant church of a different kind in England, was the work which God sent John Knox into the world to do; and he spent his life in doing this work.

3. *The character of Knox.* Some people find fault with John Knox because he was a rough man; but we must remember that he had rough people to deal with and

rough work to do; and if he had not been a stern, rugged man himself, he would hardly have been fit to do the work he had to do; but with all this, he was a great and good man. There were three things about him that helped to make him such. In the first place he had great good sense. He knew what was the right thing to do, and the right time for doing it. Some people never find out what they ought to do till it is too late to do it. It was not so with Knox.

And then he understood people as well as things. Queen Mary tried to deceive him, but she could not do it. He seemed to read and understand her as he would a book. This was a great help to him in the work he had to do, and it was an important part of his character.

And then he had great courage as well as great good sense. When they were standing around his grave at his funeral, the Earl of Morton, one of the chief noblemen of Scotland, and who had known Knox intimately, pointed to his coffin, and said: "There lies one who never feared the face of man." When doing his duty, he never cared for kings, or queens, or priests, or princes, or popes. He feared God alone, and so he found the truth of what is taught us in the hymn which tells us of God, and says,

> "Fear him ye saints, and you will then
> Have nothing else to fear."

This is an important element of character for all great and good men.

Then John Knox had great piety, as well as great good sense and courage. Love to Jesus is the root out of which all true piety springs. Paul said, "The love of Christ constraineth us." This was the secret of Paul's greatness. So it was with John Knox as it is with all true Christians. Let us thank God for the life, and work, and character of Knox, and let us pray that we may have the same good sense and courage and piety which made up the character of the great and good John Knox.

Zwingli and Luther.

CHAPTER XXI.

ULRICH ZWINGLI. 1484–1531.

WE will now return to the Continent, and continue our history of the Reformation there. Switzerland is a little country, but it is a very famous one.

The great Swiss hero of the Reformation was Ulrich Zwingli. What we have to say of him may be said in connection with *his birth, his character, and his death.*

1. *The birth of Zwingli.* He was born in a little mountain village called Toggenburg, in Switzerland. Luther was born on the 1st of November, 1483, and Zwingli on January 1, 1484. And so we see that these two great men began their lives very near together. Luther was only two months older than Zwingli. His father was a shepherd, a poor man, but very

much beloved and respected by all who knew him. He had a large family of eight sons and two daughters, and of these ten children Ulrich was the third. In his early boyhood, like David on the plains of Bethlehem, he kept his father's sheep. His mother used to tell him stories from the Bible, while his father told him stories connected with the history of Switzerland, and so a love for the Bible and a love for his native land, or piety and patriotism grew up together in his heart.

He went to school at Basle when he was ten years old, where he met with learned men, and among them the famous Erasmus. He was an earnest and diligent student, and was greatly beloved by his teachers. He next studied some time in Berne and also in Vienna. During all this time he was an earnest student of the Greek Testament, and it was while thus simply studying the pure word of God, that his eyes were opened to see the many errors that were prevailing in the church of Rome, and which made it so necessary that there should be a reformation.

In the year 1506, when he was twenty-two years of age, he was ordained by the Bishop of Constance, and was placed in charge of a large church not far from his native town. These were the most important matters connected with his birth and education.

2. *The character of Zwingli.* He was a a *Bible loving man.* We have seen how diligently he studied it while he was at school and college. And when he became a priest he still continued to do so. He not only read and studied the scriptures, but committed them to memory. He did this with all the New Testament, and then did the same with large portions of the Old Testament. In the first sermon that he preached, on taking charge of the congregation with whom he labored for ten years, he said, "To Christ will I lead you as the source of salvation. His word is the only food I wish to furnish to your hearts and lives." This was the true bread of life, while the priests generally in those days fed the people with chaff.

He was an independent man. When he

found out what the Bible taught, he did not stop to ask what Luther or any other great man thought about this teaching, but began at once to preach to the people just what he learned from the Bible. When some one said to him, "Master Ulrich, they tell me you have gone into the new error, and that you must certainly be a Lutheran;" his reply was, "I learned the doctrines that I preach from the Greek Testament, before I ever heard the name of Luther. I preach also as Paul writes; why do you not then call me a Paulinian? Yes, I preach the word of Christ; why do you not rather call me a Christian.

On the subject of the Lord's Supper, Zwingli and Luther held very different views. In the year 1529, a great conference was held at Marburg, between these two good men and their friends, to talk this matter over and see if they could not agree to hold the same views about it. They had a long argument but neither could convince the other that he was wrong. But they separated as friends, and agreed to differ in love where they could not think alike.

3. *The death of Zwingli.* He died in battle, not as a soldier but as a chaplain. His country was engaged in warfare. He was ordered to go with one of the regiments, not to fight, but to comfort the sick and wounded and to prepare them for death. After one of the battles he was kneeling down over a wounded soldier and telling him about Jesus, when a stone struck him on the head and made him senseless. Soon after he rose to his feet, when a spear was thrust into him, from the wound of which he died, when he was only forty-seven years old. Like John the Baptist he was great, not from the length of his life but from its devotion to God.

CHAPTER XXII.

JOHN CALVIN. 1509–1564.

GENEVA is a celebrated city in Europe. It was the home of Calvin, another great Swiss Reformer, and it is famous for

1. *The beauty of its situation.* Look at the picture. Directly in front you see a river, with a bridge across it. This is the river Rhone, or rather one of its branches, as it flows out from Lake Geneva. The water is very clear, and rushes by very rapidly. In the middle of the river, on the left hand side of the bridge, is a little island. It is nicely shaded by trees and lighted up with gas, and on summer evenings they have concerts and musical entertainments there. Along the banks of the river, on the other side, you see a row of fine, large buildings. These are hotels and stores. There is a similar row

View of Geneva. The home of Calvin.

of buildings on this side of the river. The large building with three short, pointed towers rising up from it, over on the other side of the city, is the cathedral church of St. Peter, in which Calvin, the great Reformer, used to preach. The mountains represented as covered with snow, seem to be very near, but yet they are sixty miles distant. The highest mountain to be seen from Geneva is the celebrated Mount Blanc, which is the highest mountain in Switzerland or in Europe except some peaks in the Caucasus. These mountains can only be seen from Geneva when the sky is very clear.

The Lake of Geneva, at the western end of which the city stands, is about fifty miles long, and from four to eight or nine miles wide. In some places it is as much as a thousand feet deep. The water is remarkably clear and crystal-like, and its color, as you look at it in the lake, is a beautiful deep blue. As you stand and gaze at the deep blue of the sky above, and then at the lake beneath, of just the same color, it seems, for all the world, as if a portion of the sky had fallen down into the lake.

There is one thing about this lake which is very interesting. At the opposite end of the lake from that on which Geneva stands, the river Rhone flows into it. The waters of this river are nearly all supplied by the melting snows which flow down from the mountains of Switzerland. The effect of this is that as this river enters the lake, its waters are thick and muddy. For a while it flows on through this beautiful lake without apparently receiving any benefit from it. But before it gets through the lake, all the muddiness of this river is gone, and as it flows out from the lake, its waters are all pure and sparkling and beautiful. What a good illustration we have here of our Sunday-school work. Compare a Sunday-school to the Lake of Geneva, with its beautifully clear waters. Compare some of the boys and girls who enter the school, in their ignorance and sin, to the muddy waters of the river Rhone as it enters the lake. For a while they seem to get no good from the school, but by and by they learn about Jesus. They begin to pray to him. His truth enlightens their minds. His blood washes away their sins. His grace renews their hearts. They become "new creatures in Christ Jesus," faithful followers of the loving Saviour. And when they leave the school, the change which has come over them is as great as that seen in the river Rhone, as its sparkling waters flow out in their purity from Geneva's beautiful lake.

2. *Geneva and the Reformation.* The most interesting thing in the history of Geneva is its intimate connection with the great work of the Reformation. Martin Luther had no firmer friend or abler helper in carrying on the work to which he gave his life than he found in John Calvin. Many other good and noble men labored in this cause in Geneva, but the most useful and famous of them all was Calvin. He was a great preacher and a great writer. We cannot tell how many books he wrote altogether. I have between fifty and sixty large volumes of his writings in

my library, and these are only a portion of them. Most of the books that he wrote are commentaries on the Bible. He was a very good and very learned man. And though he held views about certain doctrines in which some do not agree with him, yet most people are thankful for the opportunity of reading his books, and of learning from them to understand more clearly the precious truth that God has taught us in his holy word. Calvin was a splendid example for all young people to follow, in his industry, in his perseverance, his courage, and his simplicity. By the many labors and sacrifices of his life, he has caused his name to be connected with the history and glory of Geneva in a way that must remain as long as the city stands.

Now let us look at some features in the life and character of Calvin.

How interesting it would be if we knew how many souls were brought to Jesus and saved, through God's blessing on the humble labors of John Calvin!

Calvin lived about three hundred years

ago.* He was one of the most useful and active of the Reformers. He was remarkable for three things. In each of these things every young person would do well by following his example.

1. Calvin was an example of *youthful diligence.* He had been so earnest and diligent in his studies, that when he was only twenty-two years of age, it was said by one who knew him well, and who was

* John Calvin was born at Noyon in Picardy about 70 miles northeast of Paris, July 10, 1509, and died in Geneva May 27, 1564. His father was poor, but secured the best educational advantages, and he became chaplain of the chapel de la Gesìne, when only 12 years old. In 1523 he went to Paris to prepare for the priesthood, was curate at Marteville and Pont l' Eveque 1527–1529. In 1527 at the advice of his father he studied law, attending lectures at Orleans and Bourges, and lecturing at the former place in the absence of the professor. While at Bourges, he studied with Andreas Alciati, then the most distinguished law professor in Europe, and learned Greek and Protestant doctrines under Wolmar. Calvin returned to Paris to continue theology in 1532; wrote an address for Cop, advocated reform in the Catholic church, and was compelled to flee to the south of France, wandering for two years under assumed names to escape persecution. At Angouleme he began to prepare his *Institutes of Religion*, which he finally published in Latin at Basle, in 1536; came to Geneva the same year, where he preached and labored for the Reformation with great earnestness along with Farel and other Reformers, until his death in 1564.—E. W. R.

a good judge, that he was the most learned person in Europe. He understood the value of time, and he improved it well. He knew that moments were like gold dust, worth more than diamonds. He gathered them up carefully, and let none slip away unimproved. And this is one of the surest secrets of success. Solomon knew very well what he was about when he made such statements as these: "Whatsoever thy hand findeth to do, do it with thy might" (Eccl. 9:10). "Seest thou a man diligent in his business? he shall stand before kings; he shall not stand before mean men" (Prov. 22:29). And Calvin's life shows clearly the honor and blessing that follow such youthful diligence.

2. Calvin was an example of *patient industry*. He must have been one of the busiest men that ever lived. For the last twenty years of his life, it is said that he preached every day; lectured three times a week; attended the business meetings of the church, and yet found time to write letters to persons in several parts of the

world; and to be making books all the time. Besides his printed books, there are more than two thousand of his written sermons, that are preserved in the library at Geneva.

I cannot tell how many volumes he published. Some time ago, a society was formed in England, called "The Calvin Translation Society." The object of this society was to get his books, which were written in Latin and French, translated and printed in English. *Fifty-one large volumes* of Calvin's works have been published by this society. These volumes make a library in themselves. How busy he must have been! And yet he was not a strong man either. His health was feeble, and he was only fifty-five years old when he died. When we hear or read of Calvin, let us remember his *patient industry*, and try to imitate his example in this respect.

3. And then Calvin was an example of *Christian liberality*. He worked so hard, and made so many books, which had an extensive sale, that people used to say of

him, that he was laying up money and getting rich. But this was not the case. He gave away his money so freely to relieve the poor, and to help do good in various ways, that when he died, although he had lived in the simplest, plainest way —and often took only one meal a day— yet all the money he left behind was about two hundred and fifty dollars. He was indeed laying up treasure all the time: but then he was laying it up, not on earth, but in heaven. This is the best use to make of money; it will pay the best in the end, for it will be yielding us interest all through eternity.

Let every reader try to imitate the example of John Calvin in his *youthful diligence*, his *patient industry*, and his *Christian liberality*.

Angouleme, in France. Calvin's Retreat.

CHAPTER XXIII.

ANGOULEME. 1537.

ANGOULEME is an interesting city on several accounts, and especially for its relation to the Reformation.

It is a very ancient city. Angouleme was founded in the early part of the Christian era. As far back as the sixth century an old hermit came to this place and introduced Christianity. The people there point out an old grotto in which that hermit lived, and so for its antiquity Angouleme is an interesting place.

It is interesting again for its *position.* It is situated on a hill near the river Charente, in a province of the same name, in the southwest part of France. Its surroundings are very beautiful, and the fine old buildings belonging to it, must add greatly to the interest of its appearance. And then, in its history this fine old town is full of interest.

Angouleme was the birthplace of Marguerite de Valois, the queen of Navarre, and sister of Francis I., the celebrated king of France. She was one of the most famous women of the age in which she lived. She had an excellent education and spoke several languages. She wrote beautiful poetry, and published a number of books that were very valuable. She took a lively interest in the cause of the Reformation, and deserves to be numbered among the friends of that great cause. We cannot call her one of the *heroes* of the Reformation; but as a heroine she well deserves to take her place among them.

1. *She was an example of sympathy.* At one time her brother, Francis I., the king of France, was engaged in war with Charles V., the emperor of Spain. In one of the battles of that war Francis was defeated and made prisoner. Charles had him taken to Madrid, the capital of

Spain, and there put him in prison. Marguerite heard of her brother's imprisonment, and that he was taken sick in prison. This distressed her very much; she could not rest day or night for thinking of her sick and suffering brother. Her sympathy for him was so great that she finally made up her mind to go to him and try to do what she could to help and comfort him. And in those days, when there were no railroads or public conveyances of any kind, to go from Paris to Madrid, from the capital of France to the capital of Spain, was a long and dangerous and expensive journey. But Marguerite did not allow the thought of the time it would take, or the danger and expense it would involve, to weigh with her a moment. She started on that long journey, she reached the end of it in safety, she visited her brother in prison, she comforted him in his trouble, she nursed him through his sickness, and then she appealed to the emperor Charles V. for the release of her brother. The appeal was successful; her brother was released, and permitted to return to his kingdom. How noble this was in Marguerite de Valois! And if we have the same sympathy for those who are in suffering, it will make us like angels of mercy wherever we may be.

2. *She had courage.* John Calvin was one of the most learned and active and useful ministers of the Protestant church at that time. The authorities of the Romish church at Paris were very angry with him. They passed a decree compelling him to leave the country, and threatened him with imprisonment and death. He left his home in disguise, intending to make his way into Switzerland. His journey led him to Angouleme. He stayed there awhile. When Marguerite heard of it, she persuaded him to remain there, and showed him every possible kindness. She wrote to her brother, the king, and persuaded him to have the persecution of Calvin stopped. This was done, and it was just here that Marguerite's courage showed itself. She knew that the authorities of the Romish church in Paris were very angry with her on account of the

help she had given to the Protestants. They had already threatened to have her sewed up in a bag and thrown into the river. She knew that the kindness she was now showing to Calvin would make them more angry still; but she did not mind it; she only asked herself, "Is it a right thing that I am doing?" When satisfied on this point she went on and did it, and left the result with God. He will always bless those who, like this noble woman, have courage to do what they know is right, and then leave it with him.

3. *She was an example of practical piety.* Her religion did not spend itself in merely going regularly to church and engaging in public services. She did this faithfully; but then she felt that this was not all she had to do. Between the times when those public services were held she was persuaded that she ought to follow the example of her blessed Saviour, who "went about doing good," and she did so. The queen of Navarre though she was, she yet spent a large portion of her time in visiting the homes of the poor, and sup-

plying the wants of the sick in her neighborhood. She would not only send them relief by her servants, but would go herself, in person, to visit and comfort them in their sorrow, and to read and talk to them about that blessed Saviour who came down from heaven to seek and to save them that are lost. It is very interesting to think of one in her high position carrying out her religion in this way. And here she sets us all a good example.

Let us remember her *sympathy*, her *courage*, and her *practical piety*, and then let us try to "follow her, as she followed Christ."

CHAPTER XXIV.

WILLIAM FAREL. 1489–1565.

FAREL was a co-worker with Calvin in the great Reformation. We owe the great Reformers a debt of gratitude that we can never pay.

What a privilege it is that we can open our Bibles whenever we wish, and read therein about the wonderful works of God! We owe this privilege to what those good men did. If it had not been for the Reformation we should not have been allowed to read the Bible.

What a privilege it is that we can go to Sunday-school, and to church, and hear the blessed gospel of Jesus taught and preached to us; and that we can worship God in the way that we think best! We should not have had this privilege if it had not been for the Reformation.

The Rev. William Farel was a learned and faithful minister of the gospel, who lived about three hundred years ago, and helped on the great work of the Reformation in France and Switzerland.* There were two things in his character, which we may well try to imitate; and one, not so good, which we should try to avoid.

1. *Farel was a brave man.* When God taught him to understand the gospel, he preached it boldly, although he knew there was great danger in doing so. The pope of Rome and his bishops and priests were busily engaged at that time in persecuting and putting into prison and to death those who preached the doctrines of the Reformation. But Farel, like Luther, and Calvin, and the other brave Reformers, never hesitated about doing his

* William Farel was born at Gap, in Dauphiny, 1489. He studied in Paris, became professor of a college, went to Basle, was expelled because of his advocacy of Reform doctrines, returned to Switzerland, preached in various parts of that country, making journeys over the mountains in his labors, settled in Geneva in 1532, was expelled with Calvin in 1538, went to Neufchatel, Metz and Gorze, from whence he fled in disguise, to escape being massacred by catholic troops, and died in Neufchatel September 15, 1565.—E. W. R.

duty on account of the danger to which it exposed him. When they persecuted him in one place, according to our Saviour's command, he fled to another. But he never gave up his work on this account. He never stopped preaching.

Courage or bravery is a fine thing in a soldier. He is worth nothing without it. And if we wish to be "good soldiers of Jesus Christ," we must be brave as Farel was. And if we are loving and serving Jesus, we may well be brave in all that we know to be right, for we know that he will take care of us and not let anything harm us.

2. *Farel was a self-denying man.* If he had desired to live an easy, quiet life, without exposing himself to dangers, or trials, or persecutions of any kind, he could have done so by simply giving up the cause for which the Reformers worked, and remaining in the Romish church. But his desire was to do what was right in the sight of God, and not what would be the easiest for himself. It was no easy thing to travel over the Swiss mountains

at any time, but especially in the depths of winter. Yet Farel never hesitated to go when duty called him. He was always ready to deny himself for the glory of God, and for the good of men. And this is the true spirit of a Christian. Jesus said, "If any man will be my disciple, let him *deny himself*, and take up his cross daily, and follow me." Let us all try to have a self-denying spirit.

But there was one thing about Farel that was not so good. I mention this not that we should try to imitate it, but that we should avoid it.

3. *Farel was a hot tempered man.* He was something like the disciples when they wanted their Master to let them call down fire from heaven, as Elijah did, on those who would not do what they wished. One day he saw a Romish procession going along the street. He went up to the priest, who was carrying an image of St. Anthony, snatched the image out of his hands and threw it into the river. This raised a great tumult, and Farel came near losing his life. It was wrong

for him to do this. It was not what our blessed Lord would have advised him to do. One of his friends, a leading man among the reformers, reproved him for this violence.

"Remember, brother," he said, "men may be led by gentleness, but they will not be driven by violence. Do not forget that you were sent to *preach* to people, but not to *rail* at them. Pour on wine and oil in due season, and try to act as a loving minister of Christ, but not as a task master or a tyrant." This was good advice for him, and it is good advice to us. Jesus said, "Learn of me, for *I am meek and lowly in heart.*" Let us strive to imitate "the gentleness of Christ." In the language of the hymn let us each be constantly saying:

"Rest for my soul I long to find;
Saviour of all, if mine thou art,
Give me thy meek and lowly mind,
And stamp thine image on my heart."

CHAPTER XXV.

JOHN ALASCO, THE POLISH REFORMER.

1499–1560.

WHO was John Alasco? you ask. We never heard of him. When we hear about the Reformation, we always think of Luther, and Calvin, and Zwingli, and Cranmer, and Knox, and other great and good men whom God raised up to help them in their important work. Some of these men, though very useful in their day, are not so well known as those we have just named. John Alasco,* one of the Reformers, is not so well known as some others are, and this is the reason why we introduce him to our young friends, and desire to tell them something about him.

And there are three things of which we wish to speak in connection with this good

* He is sometimes called John à Lasco or Jan Laski.

man. These are: *his birth and education, his sacrifices for the Reformation*, and *his travels and labors.*

1. *Alasco's birth and education.* He was born in the year 1499, the last year of the fifteenth century. He belonged to one of the richest and most honorable families in Poland. One of his uncles was the leading man connected with the Romish church in Poland. He occupied the office of archbishop. The family and friends of Alasco wished him to enter the church and become a priest. He was educated for this office, and no pains were spared to secure for him the best education that could be had in those days.

After learning all that could be taught him in his own country, he was sent abroad to finish his education. He went first to France and then to Switzerland. Here he became acquainted with Zwingli, the famous Swiss Reformer, and with Erasmus, who was celebrated for his learning. From these good men he learned many things which led the way to his joining the cause of the Reformation, as he did afterwards.

2. *Alasco's sacrifices for the Reformation.* He was called back to his own country by his friends, and especially his uncle the archbishop. He was unwilling to have him stay any longer in Switzerland, being afraid of the influence which the friends of the Reformation there might have upon him. But what they considered *the evil* had already been done. He had been studying the scriptures. David says, "The entrance of thy words giveth light" (Ps. 119 : 130). And it was so in Alasco's case. God's Word had entered his mind and heart. And its entrance gave him light. As that light was shining around him, he began to see the difference between the doctrines taught by the church of Rome and those that the Bible taught.

But he did not quit the church of Rome and join the Reformers at once. The truth of God had enlightened his mind, but it had not yet taken full possession of his heart. His family and friends belonged to the Romish church, and all his prospects of succeeding in worldly affairs seemed to lie in that direction. He saw that there were many things contrary to the scriptures in the church of Rome, still he hoped, as many other good men did in those days, that these errors might be reformed in the old church without making a new one. And so he became a priest, and entered earnestly on the duties of that office.

After a while the offer was made to him of becoming a bishop in the church. Indeed he had his choice between two offices of this kind. One of these was the most important place in the country for a bishop to occupy. If he had taken this position, he would on the death of his uncle, be the archbishop of Poland. This was the highest honor he could have in connection with the Romish church in that country. It was a splendid prospect for this world to set before a young man.

And what did Alasco do? He made up his mind not to accept this tempting offer. The fact was that after becoming a priest in the Romish church, and finding out what wicked men most of the priests were, what bad doctrines they taught, and what wicked lives they lived, he saw it would be impossible to reform such a corrupt church by staying in it. He then made up his mind that he must go out of it. As soon as he came to this conclusion, he went to the king of Poland, who was his friend, and told him frankly and bravely how he felt. He thanked him for the offer he had made him of becoming a bishop, and said that he felt it to be his duty to leave the church of Rome and join the Reformed church. This was noble in him. It was going through the same sort of trial that Moses had to meet, when, as Paul says, he "refused to be called the son of Pharaoh's daughter; choosing rather to suffer affliction with the people of God, than to enjoy the pleasures of sin for a season; esteeming the reproach of Christ greater riches than the treasures of Egypt" (Heb. 11 : 24, 25). This was a noble act for John Alasco to perform.

3. *Alasco's travels and labors.* As soon as he made up his mind to leave the Romish church, he found his position so uncomfortable that he concluded to leave his native country, and go to live and and labor for Christ in strange lands. First he went to Holland, and labored there a while. After this Archbishop Cranmer invited him to England, to help in finishing the work of the Reformation. There he had charge of a large congregation of foreigners, who, like himself, had fled to England for refuge from the persecution to which they were exposed in their own countries. There he was very useful, and would probably have spent the rest of his life; but when King Edward VI. died, his sister Mary became queen of England. She was a bigoted Romanist, and began at once to persecute the Reformers. So fierce was her persecution that it has gained for her the name of "*Bloody Mary*," as we have seen. Then Alasco had to leave England. He went back to his own country. In the meantime the cause of the Reformation had

grown there. The king was favorable to it, and Alasco was appointed superintendent of the Reformed churches in part of Poland. The rest of his life was spent in this work. By his preaching, by his counsel, and by his writings, he was of the greatest possible help to this good cause.

Reading the Protest at Spires.

CHAPTER XXVI.

THE PROTEST AT SPIRES. 1529.

THE most important and interesting event in connection with the Reformation was the "Protest at Spires."

1. *The place referred to.* Speyer or Spires is an interesting old town in that part of Germany called Bavaria. It is situated on the river Rhine, and is one of the oldest towns in Germany. It formerly had a population of nearly thirty thousand people, but now the number of its inhabitants is only about thirteen thousand. It is a walled town, with gates and towers. There used to be a large palace here belonging to the emperors of Germany, and here they lived a great part of the time. This palace is now in ruins. There is also a very large cathedral here, and in the vaults under the cathedral many of the

emperors and other great persons are buried. In this city of Spires the great council, which the Germans called diet, used to be held. And it is one of these councils or diets, and the most important ever held there, which we will describe.

2. *The Protest.* This diet or council was called together by the Emperor Charles V., in the year 1529. The Emperor himself did not attend the meeting. He sent his brother Ferdinand to take his place. And when the members of the diet met, the Emperor's letter was read, telling them what he wanted them to do. It was a very short letter. There was only one thing he wished them to attend to. This was to repeal the law which had been passed at the meeting of the diet three years before, in 1526. To repeal a law is to undo it, or make it cease to be a law. The law here referred to was one that gave religious liberty to Germany, by allowing people to worship God in the way they thought best. This law had been passed by the friends of Luther. It was intended to protect persons from be-

ing punished if they wished to join the Reformed Church. It was a great help to the cause of the Reformation. This cause had spread so rapidly, and such great numbers of people had joined it, that the pope and the leaders of the Romish church were greatly alarmed. They felt that they must do something to stop the Reformation from spreading. This lead them to urge the Emperor to call a meeting of the diet for this purpose. When the meeting was opened, the Emperor's brother Ferdinand tried to get a resolution passed to set aside the law which secured religious freedom, and to forbid any one to preach or hold the doctrines of Luther under pain of imprisonment or death. But the German princes, who were the friends of Luther and the Reformation, opposed this so strongly that it could not be done.

Then the friends of the pope concluded to say no more about that. But they proposed to pass a resolution that whatever a man's religion was, he should cling to it and make no change. This seemed fair, and it was passed. But the German princes, who loved the Reformation, met together to consult about it. They saw at once that this resolution was intended to prevent the Reformation from spreading any further. So they agreed to write a protest against it. And before the meeting of the diet was over, the Elector of Saxony, the greatest of the princes, was requested to read it before the diet. And this he did. Ferdinand had left the meeting, and had gone home as soon as the resolution was passed. And so his chair which he had occupied was empty when this protest was read. And this is what was done at the diet of Spires.

3. *The importance of this act.* It was important for two things. One was this, *it showed how noble was the spirit of those German princes!* If they had been selfish men, they might have said, "Well, this does not prevent us from holding to the reformed religion ourselves, and so we are satisfied. We will say nothing against what the diet has done." But they were not selfish men. They thought of others

as well as of themselves. They saw that this resolution was intended to prevent other persons from joining the Reformed church, however much they might wish to do so. And so, like good, brave, noble men as they were, they took their stand in favor of religious liberty. For this they deserve our thanks, and are worthy of all honor.

And then this action was important *because it gave to the friends of the Reformation the name which they have always borne since then.* This is what the word *Protestant* comes from. The brave men who made this *protest* were the first to be called *Protestant.* And so for more than three hundred years this name has been applied to all who love the doctrines of the Reformation. Thank God for the noble men who made this protest at the diet of Spires!

CHAPTER XXVII.

WILLIAM THE SILENT. 1533–1584.

WILLIAM THE SILENT was one of the best and greatest men that ever lived. He died three hundred years ago. He was born in Germany, in the year 1533, and died in 1584, when he was only fifty-one years of age. He was the founder of the Republic of Holland. Holland is a very small country. Much of the land belonging to it has been recovered from the sea, and the waters of the sea are only kept from flowing over it by walls or banks of mud and earth, which the people build and keep up with great toil and labor. But the Hollanders, the people who live in this little country, are manly, and brave, and intelligent, and pious. Their history is one of the most interesting of any of the nations of the earth. There have

William the Silent.

been many good and great men belonging to this country, but this man was the greatest of them all. He was called "William the Silent" because he was a man of very few words. He believed in *acting* rather than in *talking*. He is sometimes called "William of Nassau," because this was the name of the place where he lived; and sometimes he is called "William, Prince of Orange," because this was the name of the family to which he belonged.

He was more like our own great Washington than any other man of whom we read in history. We may speak of William the Silent and Washington in the way of comparison and of contrast. There are *three* things in which they were alike, and so in these we may compare them. There is *one* thing in which they were unlike, and in this they may be contrasted.

1. *William and Washington were alike in their characters.* They were both *brave* men. When the good of his country required it, William was not afraid to fight against Philip II., king of Spain,

although he was then the mightiest monarch in the world. And Washington, when the good of his country required it, was not afraid to fight against George III., king of England, when England was undoubtedly one of the most powerful countries on the globe.

They were both *wise* men. William the Silent never gained great and splendid victories like those which Alexander and Napoleon gained, and yet he managed to hold out against the strongest armies that Spain could send against him. This shows how wise he was. And it was just the same with Washington. He managed to keep on fighting for seven long years, against all the armies that England could send to this country, till England got tired of the business and concluded to give it up. This shows how wise he was.

And then they were both *pious* men. William was a Roman Catholic in his younger days, but when he found that the Spaniards were trying to set up the horrible Inquisition in Holland, and to torture and burn the people just because they wanted to read their Bibles and to worship God according to their own consciences, he gave up being a Romanist and became a Protestant. He had faith in God, and he prayed to God to help him in his struggles for his country. William the Silent was a man of piety and of prayer. And so was Washington. He never was a Romanist like William, and never had to contend against them as he did. But he had faith in God as the God of nations, as William had. He was not ashamed to acknowledge God as the one in whom he trusted, and to pray to him for help while fighting for his country. They were both brave men, both wise men, both pious men.

2. *William and Washington were alike in fighting for their country.* The people of Holland were few and weak compared with the people of Spain. Yet when William saw that Spain was trying to oppress his countrymen and take away their liberties from them, he resolved, whatever it might cost him, to stand by them in their struggle, and fight on till they gained their liberty.

And so it was with Washington. He saw that the king of England was doing wrong to the people of this country, and taking away their liberties, and he resolved to join with them in their efforts to throw off the rule of England and to establish their independence. William the Silent succeeded in making Holland independent of Spain, and so did Washington succeed in making this country independent of England.

3. *William was greatly beloved by his people, and so was Washington.* The people of Holland were so fond of William that they used to speak of him as "Father William." He had been like a father to them, and they had all the affection of children towards him. And so it was with Washington. He was called the "Father of his country." No man was ever more loved and honored by any people than Washington was by the people of this country. It used to be said of him, and it was said truly, that he was "first in war, first in peace, and first in the hearts of his countrymen."

In the three things spoken of, William the Silent and Washington may well be compared with each other. They were alike in these things. But there is one thing in which they were unlike each other. They may be contrasted here.

4. *William and Washington were unlike in their death.* William died by the hand of an assassin. The king of Spain put a price upon his head, that is, he offered a large sum of money to any one who would kill him. A miserable wretch came to his palace one day under pretence of asking a favor from him, and while this noble prince was going down stairs to see him, the worthless fellow took out a pistol and shot him dead.

But Washington died a natural death. No hand of violence was raised against him. After a short but severe illness, at his own quiet home at Mount Vernon, on the banks of the Potomac, and in the presence of his distressed and sorrowing family, the great man calmly finished his earthly course and entered into "the rest that remaineth for the people of God."

CHAPTER XXVIII.

NICHOLAS, THE LAY PREACHER. 1540.

MORE than three hundred years ago, there was a young man in Holland who preached a gospel sermon. It was when Martin Luther and his friends were trying to make known to those about them the great truths of the Bible. This was the way in which they hoped to save people from the errors that were taught by the Romish priests. There was nothing those priests were more afraid of than the Bible. They tried in every way to keep people from becoming acquainted with that blessed book and its teachings. In the city of Antwerp they persecuted and put to death those who attempted to preach the gospel to the people. They offered a reward to every one who would give them notice of persons who were preaching the gospel.

Those persons would immediately be taken up and be thrown into prison or put to death. And so it was as much as a man's life was worth in those days to attempt to tell "the old, old story of Jesus and his love." And yet, even in those days, there were numbers of people who longed to hear the gospel, and in unexpected ways God raised up persons to preach it.

One Sunday a great crowd of people met together on one of the wharves by the river Scheldt in Antwerp. They wanted to hear about the Bible, and they hoped that some good minister would come and preach to them. No minister came. Still they waited. Among that crowd there was a young man named Nicholas. He was not a minister, but God had taught him to know and love the Bible. He made up his mind to give those people a plain Bible talk. So he stepped on the deck of a vessel in the river. There he stood up, and taking out his Bible he read the account of Christ feeding the multitude with five loaves and two fishes. And then he gave them a good, plain, earnest sermon on the subject. The people were delighted to hear him.

But some one went and told the priests that Nicholas was preaching the gospel to the people. They resolved to stop him from preaching. So they hired two wicked men to make way with him. These men met him in the street. They seized him, bound him hand and foot, put him in a sack, tied up the sack, and threw him into the river, and drowned him.

If we had been living in those days how hard it would have been for us to learn anything about Jesus and his salvation! How little we should have known of the Bible! But how much of it we know now! When we think of the people who were living in those days, and then think of ourselves, of our Bibles, and Sabbath-schools, and ministers, and teachers, and books, and papers, all telling us of Jesus, and what he has done for our salvation, surely it should teach us *a lesson of thankfulness!*

CHAPTER XXIX.

THE DUKE OF ALVA. 1568.

THE Duke of Alva was a bad man. He lived in the Reformation times, though he was not one of the "Heroes of the Reformation." He had a great deal to do with the Reformation, but it was only in the way of *hindering* and not of *helping* it.

He was born in the year 1508 of a noble Spanish family. He early became a soldier, and spent a long life as a famous and successful general, doing good service in the interest of the Spanish government. But, so far as the work of the Reformation was concerned, he did more to injure it than any other man then living. He persecuted the Protestants, condemning them to prison and to death by hundreds and by thousands.

The Duke of Alva, as he went from place to place, would send for the principal persons of the town or country, and make them give a solemn pledge over the sign of the cross not to favor the cause of the Protestants in any way.

The Duke of Alva was the worst enemy the Reformers ever had; and he was the most successful too. He defeated the Protestants in battle. He drove the Prince of Orange, the best friend of the Protestants, out of his country. He went through the Netherlands, from town to town, imprisoning the best people in every place, and putting them to death. During the six years of his rule he caused nearly 20,000 people to be executed. And this was done too in the most cruel ways. Men were shot, were beheaded, were hung by the neck or with the head downward, they were broken on the wheel, were slowly roasted to death, were buried alive, were starved, were torn to death with red-hot pincers. And he did this year after year. How strange and mysterious this was! No one can explain it now.

He had an army in the Netherlands for the purpose of persecuting the Protestants and trying to stop the spread of the Reformation. He was making great progress in this work, and it really seemed as though he would succeed in carrying the whole country back to the teaching of the church of Rome. Then William, Prince of Orange, who was the true ruler of that country, but who had been obliged to flee to Holland to save his life, resolved to see what he could do for the relief of his country. So he raised an army and marched into the Netherlands to fight with the Duke of Alva. But the duke had made up his mind not to fight with the prince. He changed his position twenty-nine times to avoid engaging in battle. There were two reasons why he was unwilling to fight with the Prince of Orange. One was, he was afraid that if the battle was once begun it would excite the Netherlanders to engage in the conflict, and then he would be defeated. The other reason was, he knew that the Prince of Orange had very little money, because all his property in the Netherlands had been taken from him. He felt sure that the prince would not be able to pay his soldiers their wages, and then they would soon become discontented and desert his standard and go home. Thus he saw that a little delay would secure him a greater victory over the prince than he could expect to gain by fighting him. And it turned out just so. The army of the Prince of Orange soon deserted him. Then he was obliged to give up any further effort for the good of his country, and retire to private life in Holland. This shows us that, bad man as the Duke of Alva was, he yet had great practical wisdom. There is an old saying that "the better part of valor is discretion." There never was a better illustration of this than we find in this part of the Duke of Alva's conduct.

The Duke of Alva was not given to showing kindness. He was one of the most hard-hearted and cruel men that ever lived. This is proved by his own deeds of which we have spoken. But among those he was persecuting there were some whose hearts were full of kindness.

One of the best and noblest men among the Netherlanders when Alva was carrying on his bloody persecutions was the Baron of Sterebeck. He was a very warm friend of the Reformation, and used all his influence to help on that great and good work. When the Duke of Alva heard of him he had him arrested and put in prison. Then he was tried and sentenced to be beheaded. After this he was sent back to prison, and his wife and three children were allowed to remain with him till the end came.

The day before his execution had arrived, towards the close of the day, the baron and his wife were sitting by the window of his cell feeling very sadly. As he looked through the window into the prison yard, he saw a soldier standing there, who was acting as guard. He was lifting up his long battleaxe towards the window near which the baron was standing. On the end of this weapon the baron saw a piece of paper. Leaning out of the window he picked it up. On opening it he found that it was written all over. The soldier had written it. In it he said, "At the battle of St. Quentin, as I lay on the ground wounded, my enemy was about to thrust his sword through me, when you kindly stepped forward and saved my life. You had me carried from the battle-field and carefully nursed. I have never forgotten your kindness. And now I wish to show my gratitude to you. I have arranged a plan to save your life and the lives of your family. Please follow these directions. As soon as it is dark come out of the prison. You will find the door unfastened. In the street a friend will meet you. Follow him. Round the first corner he will have two carriages in waiting. These will take you and your family to a vessel in the river which sails for England to-night. Act promptly. Your grateful friend." This plan was carried out, and the baron and his family were saved. What a beautiful illustration of the good that follows kindness!

Cordova and Prison of Inquisition.

CHAPTER XXX.

CORDOVA AND THE INQUISITION.

Cordova is a celebrated city of Spain. It is situated on a beautiful plain, on the right bank of the river Guadalquiver. Cordova is renowned for its splendid buildings, as well as for its beautiful situation. It is an ancient city, and its famous cathedral was once a Turkish mosque, when this part of Spain was in the hands of the Moors. On the right-hand side of the picture is a building in ruins. This is the remains of one of the prisons of the Romish Inquisition. The Inquisition was a sort of a religious court composed of bishops and priests appointed by the pope, and formed in the principal cities of Europe before the time of the Reformation. Their business was to bring to trial and punishment persons who were accused of heresy, or of holding doctrines contrary to those held by the church of Rome. And in speaking on this subject, we may glance first at *the work of the Inquisition*, and next at *the lessons suggested by it.*

The work of the Inquisition. The Inquisition was established in the early part of the thirteenth century, or about two hundred years before the time of the Reformation. It was set in operation in most of the large cities of Europe. In each of these cities the officers of the Inquisition had a strong prison. Now let us take an illustration of the way in which the men connected with this institution carried on their work. Let us suppose that the father of one of the first families in Cordova had been accused before the officers of the Inquisition of being a heretic; what would they do? They would send their agents for him the first night after getting this information. The agents knock at the door of the house; the question is asked, "Who's there?" "The officers of the Inquisition," is the answer given. Then they enter and make a prisoner of the head of the family. Nobody dares to say a word, or lift a finger against them. They take the poor man away and lock him up in their prison. His family will never see him again; none of them will be allowed to visit him or to write to him. Then he has to go through a sort of trial; he is charged with doing things that he never did, and with saying things that he probably never said. He denies these charges; then they torture him to make him confess. One day they would try the thumb-screw on him; this was a sort of iron glove, with loose sides, made to go on the thumb. It had a strong screw attached to it which they would turn round and keep on turning till the poor man's thumb was all crushed to a jelly; then he would be led to his cell till he got over this suffering. After this he would be taken back to the chamber of torture, and perhaps the iron boot would be tried. This was a boot made of iron, with double sides. It was put on the foot, and then iron wedges were hammered in between the sides of the boot, till the bones of the foot were all crushed.

Then, on another occasion, the poor prisoner would be taken into the torture room again; he would be stripped of his clothing, his arms and legs would be tightly bound, then he would be hung up on a hook in the ceiling, and a fire would be kindled under him to roast his feet, or the flesh would be torn from his body with red-hot pincers. These and a variety of other dreadful tortures would be inflicted on the poor prisoner, and at last he would either be condemned to be burned to death, or to be thrust into one of their miserable dungeons, where not a ray of light would ever reach him, and where he would linger on in suffering till he died of starvation. And all these horrible things were done in the name of religion and by those who professed to be the servants of God. How fearful the work of the Inquisition was! And how gladly we may turn away from this view of it, to think of some of the lessons suggested by this subject.

A lesson of thankfulness that the Inquisition is ended. For hundreds of years it went on doing its dark and bloody work. Untold thousands of good men and women suffered and died under its cruelty; but now it exists no longer. Let us thank God that the prison of the Inquisition at Cordova is in ruins. And so like prisons are, in all other places. The torture chambers are all forsaken, the thumb-screw and the iron boot and the red-hot pincers are no longer used. The dungeons are all empty, and the poor prisoners are no longer burned to death. Surely *this* is a cause for thankfulness. Suppose there was a prison of the Inquisition in Philadelphia, and one in New York, in Boston, in Chicago and in all our large cities, and that the horrible work of which we have been speaking was going on among us all the time, what a darkened shadow the thought of it would throw over our whole country! But we have nothing of the kind in all our happy land. This is certainly a cause for thankfulness.

A lesson of thankfulness to God for an open Bible. What was it which broke up the Inquisition, and let its prisons everywhere go to ruin? It was the light which shone forth from the pages of God's blessed word. Suppose that Martin Luther and the other heroes of the Reformation had never translated the Bible into the language of the different nations, and had never scattered that blessed book freely among the people, what would our condition be now? The Reformation would not have taken place. The power of the church of Rome to hold people in its bondage of superstition would never have been checked. The dreadful Inquisition would still be carrying on its horrible torture, and people would be burned to death now, by hundreds, as they used to be in those days of darkness. We never can be too thankful for that open Bible which has led to this great change. And while we rejoice in the thought of what the Bible has done for us, let us do all we can to aid in spreading it abroad everywhere. The blessing of the world is wrapped up in it. Let the language of our hearts in reference to it be:

> "Fly abroad, thou mighty gospel,
> Win and conquer, never cease;
> May thy lasting, wide dominions
> Multiply and still increase;
> Sway thy sceptre,
> Saviour! all the earth around."

CHAPTER XXXI.

ADMIRAL COLIGNI. 1572.

Coligni was one of the greatest and best men the French nation ever had. His name was Gaspard de Coligni, but generally his Christian name Gaspard was dropped. The title of the highest office that he held was applied to him, and he was known as Admiral Coligni. The position of admiral was the highest and most honorable office in the French navy. And although Coligni had been a soldier and an officer in the French army all his days, yet in reward for his many faithful services he was honored during the latter part of his life by having the title of admiral conferred upon him.

His name brings to mind a very bad deed. It was called *the Massacre of St. Bartholomew*. A massacre is a slaughter

Assassination of Coligni.

on a large scale, the killing of a great many people at once. Such a slaughter or massacre took place in the city of Paris and throughout France over three hundred years ago. It was a slaughter of Protestant Christians made by Roman Catholics, who called themselves Christians. It was called *the Massacre of St. Bartholomew* on account of the day on which it took place. This was the twenty-fourth of August, 1572. Bartholomew, you know, was one of the twelve apostles chosen by our Saviour when on earth. The Romish Church says that he suffered martyrdom or was killed for his religion on that very day, the twenty-fourth of August. So the members of that church call him St. Bartholomew, and have a religious service on the twenty-fourth of August in honor of his memory.

Charles IX. was king of France at this time. His sister was about to be married to Henry IV., king of Navarre. In honor of this wedding Charles invited great numbers of the Protestants to come to Paris, and take part in the festivities of the occasion. That they might feel quite comfortable he gave them a solemn promise of safety during their visit. Great numbers of them went, and the good admiral among them. And then that wicked king, led on by his still more wicked mother, arranged a horrible plan to have those Protestants, whom he had invited to Paris under a special promise of safety, cruelly murdered.

At two o'clock on the morning of Sunday, August 24, the bells of one of the great churches of Paris rung out its loud peals on the quiet stillness of that dark hour. This was the signal that had been agreed upon for the commencement of that dreadful massacre. Immediately the bloody work began. A band of wicked men with torches and weapons rushed into the admiral's palace. Hearing the noise of their approach, he rose to see what was the matter. On opening the door he saw at a glance what their purpose was. Addressing the leader of the band he said, "Friend, you might respect my gray hairs, but to shorten my life by a few days is all the harm you can do me." Then the wretched creature plunged his sword into the body of the good admiral, and so he died. And then through all that night and all the day following the work of slaughter went on. What a shameful thing that a deed like this should have been done on God's holy day, and been done, too, by those who called themselves Christians! It is estimated that ten thousand people were murdered in Paris on this occasion, and in other parts of France from sixty to a hundred thousand. May we not well speak of this as a *very bad deed?**

* Historical writers are not agreed in respect to the motives prompting this frightful massacre. Romanist authors generally have labored hard to prove that it was prompted by purely political, not religious influences, and that the Roman Catholic church should not be held as instigating the massacre. Some Romanists, who seek to justify religious persecution, also justify or palliate this most horrible massacre. They are certainly consistent, and have the courage of their convictions even to their strictly logical conclusions. Protestant historians agree in finding the motives leading to this wholesale massacre in accord with the uniform history and spirit of the Catholic church in those times. They point to the persecutions under Queen Mary, the horrors of the Spanish Inquisition, the bloody works of the Duke of Alva,

and to thousands of similar horrible records written in blood —the blood of those who suffered martyrdom solely because their religious views were not strictly in accord with the Romish church. Some unsuccessful efforts have recently been made to relieve that church of the odium of the St. Bartholomew massacre, and statements in an encyclopaedia have been worked over to favor an exculpation of that church. Even if this were successful there remain the vast multitude of similar cases, which are so intertwined with the history of the Reformation period that they cannot be eliminated, and the task of charging them all over to purely political influences would be too huge for any intelligent Catholic outside of an insane asylum to undertake. Catholics and Protestants alike agree that the immediate instigator of the St. Bartholomew massacre was Catharine, the mother of the reigning French monarch. She drank in the spirit of the society of the secret religious orders, and of the church in which she dwelt. Repeatedly had the Duke of Alva urged the extermination of the hated Huguenots upon Catharine, and thus on the king. To the leader of French Catholic troops she sent the order, "Take no Huguenot prisoner, but instantly kill every one!" The Catholic Alva and Philip rejoiced over the massacre. The Roman court rewarded the bearer of the news with a thousand crowns, and celebrated the event by bonfires, firing of cannon and a grand procession to the church to give thanks. The pope ordered Vàsari to paint a picture of the massacre, which was honored with a position of dignity, and the inscription, "*Pontifix Colignii necem probat*—the pope approves the murder of Coligni." Only Protestants were massacred; the Catholic was not merely safe, he was vigorously defended by the assassins if assailed by mistake. The deed is a foul blot on those pages of history which are bespattered with many similar dark deeds of persecution, which sprung from the bosom of a church which still holds that it is not necessary to keep faith with a heretic.—E. W. R.

CHAPTER XXXII.

BENJAMIN DU PLAN, THE HERO OF LANGUEDOC. 1621–1685.

LANGUEDOC was one of the provinces in the southern part of France. A large Protestant element was found there, and a very cruel persecution of the Protestants was kept up by the Roman Catholics. When the Protestants were forbidden to hold meetings in which they could worship God according to the dictates of their own consciences, great numbers of them left their homes and fled into the wild and mountainous parts of the country. And there "in dens and caves of the earth" they used to meet for the worship of God. They felt that the privilege of doing this was something which they valued far more than the comfort of their homes.

But even in those out of the way places

they were not left to themselves. The spies of the priests would follow them. They would find out where they held their meetings, and then report the same to their masters. Then soldiers would be sent out to break up those meetings, and make prisoners of the principal persons found in them.

And now let us speak of the hero of Languedoc. His name was Benjamin Du Plan. He was born in the province of Languedoc early in the seventeenth century. His father was one of the nobles of that province. He owned a large castle among the mountains, surrounded by many acres of land, and was a very wealthy man. The family were professed Protestants, but like many others they conformed to the worship of the church of Rome while the persecution was prevailing. Benjamin was their only child. He had early become acquainted with the truth as it is in Jesus. Several miles from their castle was a little mountain village in which Protestant services were held. And when the castle gates were closed at night young Du Plan was often seen climbing over the walls of the castle, and walking across the hills to attend the meeting in the village. He found great delight in listening to the simple gospel preaching there by the Huguenot ministers. He was one of the most regular attendants at those services. On one occasion he rose to speak in the meeting. He spoke with so much ease and power that the people of the village were delighted with him, and begged him to become their pastor.

He had entered the army at an early age, as was customary with young men of his position in that country. But in his twenty-second year he resolved to retire from the army and devote himself to the work of helping to spread abroad the Protestant religion.

In the year 1632 a pestilence prevailed in the province of Languedoc, and during this time our hero devoted himself to the work of visiting the sick and dying, and pointing them to Jesus as their only Saviour. During this season of sickness great seriousness prevailed among the people, and unusual numbers both of the rich as well as the poor attended the Protestant services. Something like what we should call a revival was experienced and great numbers became earnest Christians.

After this, when persecution against the Protestants began again, the Romanists tried hard to have Du Plan taked prisoner that they might put him to death. Then he was obliged to leave France and never returned to it again. He was appointed Deputy of the Reformed Churches, and spent the rest of his life in travelling through Switzerland, Holland, Germany, Denmark, Sweden and England, preaching in all those countries the glorious gospel, and trying to do all he could to help and cheer his poor persecuted countrymen.

And now in the next place let us look at *what he lost.* He lost that grand old castle which used to belong to their family. He lost his father and mother, with all the property that belonged to them.

When he had to leave his country on account of his religion, the government, after his father's death, took possession of all the family property which of right belonged to him. This was what he lost. He knew that this would be the result when he became a Protestant. It was with him as it was with the apostle Paul when he became a Christian. That step cost him "the loss of all things" he had in this world.

And now just see what this Hero of Languedoc *gained* by the course which he pursued. Who can tell what the gain of such a course will be! No one can tell it now. As the apostle says, "It doth not yet appear what we shall be." But there is one point of view from which we may look at this gain which is perfectly satisfactory. Just read what our Saviour says on this subject in Matt. 19: 29. These are his words, "Every one that hath forsaken houses, or brethren, or sisters, or father, or mother, or wife, or children, or lands, for my name's sake, shall receive a hundred-fold, and shall inherit everlasting life." This is enough. Who could desire anything more! This does not mean that the good man of whom we are speaking should receive a hundred castles in this life for the one he gave up. But it means that he should receive what would make him a hundred-fold happier in this life than ever that castle could have made him, and then, in addition to this, in the world to come he shall have everlasting life. Every one who gets that life will be satisfied. The loss which he suffered for Christ will be as nothing compared to the gain he finds in him.

Gustavus Adolphus.

CHAPTER XXXIII.

GUSTAVUS ADOLPHUS. 1592–1632.

GUSTAVUS ADOLPHUS was a famous king of Sweden. He lived more than two hundred and fifty years ago, and was one of the best and wisest kings who ever reigned over the kingdom of Sweden. It would fill a volume to tell all about his busy, useful life, and the long wars in which he was engaged. A great many important lessons might be drawn from his history. We will speak of *three*. These are lessons of great importance for all young people to learn and practice. In the life of this great man we have an excellent example of each of these lessons.

1. *An example of early industry.* Although he was the son of a king, and had a large fortune, he entered the army when he was only twelve years old. And he

did not enter it to play being a soldier, but to be a real hard-working soldier. He expected to have to spend most of his life in leading armies and fighting battles; and so he began early, and made up his mind to learn the business well. He lived, not in a palace, but in a tent like a soldier, and went through all the trying duties of a soldier's life.

And this is an example worth following; and every boy and girl should follow the example of the young king of Sweden in this respect. I do not mean that all should become soldiers as he did, but that, like him, all should early learn the lesson of industry. We should all learn not to be afraid of work.

2. *An example of early obedience.* The first thing a soldier has to do is to learn to obey. Nothing else that he can do will take the place of this. A ship that cannot sail, a gun that will not go off, or a clock that will not keep time, is good for nothing. And it is just so with a soldier who has not learned to obey.

But Gustavus Adolphus learned this

lesson well. Although he was a king's son, and expected to be king himself, there was no one in the Swedish armies more ready to obey orders than he was. And there is no more important lesson for every boy and girl to learn than this.

3. *An example of great usefulness.* There have been many kings who were of no use at all to the people over whom they reigned; but only a plague and trouble to them. It was very different, however, with the great man of whom we are now speaking. He was made king when he was only eighteen years old. He only reigned for twenty years, and then was killed in the battle of Lutzen. But during all those years he was a great blessing to his country, and to the church of God. He was an earnest Christian man, and a warm friend to the Protestants and their religion. He devoted all his time, his means and his influence to promote in every possible way the good of the country, and the glory of God. And how useful he was in both these ways it is impossible for any one to tell.

CHAPTER XXXIV.

JOHN MILTON. 1608–1674.

OLIVER CROMWELL was one of the greatest soldiers, and John Milton one of the greatest poets, that England ever knew. Milton may well be classified with the Heroes of the Reformation, for he helped on that good cause very effectively with his pen.

After the execution of Charles I., king of England, a change took place in the form of government there, and Cromwell was called to be the head of it. It was different from the monarchy which had existed in England for centuries, and entirely different from the republican government of our country. It was called a commonwealth, and Cromwell, who was at the head of the government, was called *Protector*. This new form of government lasted only during the life-time of Cromwell. While Cromwell was at the head of the English commonwealth he appointed Milton as the secretary of the government, to conduct its correspondence with other nations. In those days this correspondence was carried on in the Latin language. Milton was an excellent Latin scholar, and thus he was able to carry on this correspondence with great success. He was an earnest advocate of liberty of conscience in the worship of God; and when the church of Rome was persecuting the Waldenses and other Protestants, Milton made use of the high office which he held, and of the influence of the government which he represented, by writing to the Duke of Savoy and other officials in that part of the country, to try and have those horrible persecutions stopped. And it was while thus engaged that he was stirred up to write a celebrated sonnet on the late massacre in Piedmont, beginning,

"Avenge, O Lord, thy slaughtered saints."

There are two important lessons to be learned from Milton's life.

1. *The great secret of success in life.* Milton wrote a great many works, both in prose and poetry; but the most famous of all his writings is the great poem known as "Paradise Lost." This gives the history of the creation and fall of man. It does this in a very surprising manner. This poem of Milton's takes rank with the greatest works of poetry ever written. It is known in every land where education is enjoyed. It will last while the world stands. It shows that its author was gifted with the most marvellous poetical talent that God ever bestowed on mortal man. But did Milton trust to his great poetical talent alone to enable him to accomplish this famous work? No, for if he had he never would have succeeded in doing it. Instead of this he spent the early years of his life, and even till he reached middle age, in the most earnest and diligent study of literature and the languages. From early in the morning till late at night he gave his time and attention untiringly to study. This was the great secret of his success, and this explains

the marvellous knowledge of the English language displayed in his great poem. If he had been endowed with the gifts and talents of an angel, without the patient study of which we have spoken, he never would have been able to write such a poem as "Paradise Lost."

And what was true of Milton is true of us all. If we hope to be successful, we must be earnest and diligent in the work that is before us. We must learn to plod, and we must keep on plodding till the end before us is secured, whatever that end may be.

2. *When our work is done, wait for our reward.* Men generally expect to be paid for their work as soon as it is done. With the common laborer who depends on his wages for his support, this is natural and proper. But with our life-time labor it is very different. The reward for this does not always come in the present life. It was so with Milton in his great work "Paradise Lost." When we think how highly it is now prized, and how it has gone round the world, we might naturally

suppose that when he published this work he must have made a fortune by it. But it was not so. For the first thirteen hundred copies of his poem that were sold he received—how much do you suppose? Only five pounds of English money, or twenty-five dollars of our money. That was about a cent and a half apiece for each copy of his famous work. And after his death his daughter sold the copyright of "Paradise Lost" to the publisher for eight pounds, or forty dollars of our money. And thus we see that sixty-five dollars was all the money Milton made by his immortal work.

We who enjoy so many of the fruits of the great Reformation—an open Bible, freedom of conscience to worship God, liberty and protection in our homes, and a knowledge of the true way of salvation through our blessed Saviour alone—ought to guard zealously the principles which these great Heroes of the Reformation, under God, secured to us.

INDEX.

Other Solid Ground Titles

In addition to *Heroes of the Reformation* which you hold in your hand, Solid Ground is honored to offer many other uncovered treasure, many for the first time in more than a century:

THE CHILD AT HOME by John S.C. Abbott
THE KING'S HIGHWAY: *The 10 Commandments for the Young* by Richard Newton
THE LIFE OF JESUS CHRIST FOR THE YOUNG by Richard Newton
LET THE CANNON BLAZE AWAY by Joseph P. Thompson
THE STILL HOUR: *Communion with God in Prayer* by Austin Phelps
COLLECTED WORKS of James Henley Thornwell (4 vols.)
CALVINISM IN HISTORY *by Nathaniel S. McFetridge*
OPENING SCRIPTURE: *Hermeneutical Manual* *by Patrick Fairbairn*
THE ASSURANCE OF FAITH *by Louis Berkhof*
THE PASTOR IN THE SICK ROOM *by John D. Wells*
THE BUNYAN OF BROOKLYN: *Life & Sermons of I.S. Spencer*
THE NATIONAL PREACHER: S*ermons from 2nd Great Awakening*
FIRST THINGS: F*irst Lessons God Taught Mankind* *Gardiner Spring*
BIBLICAL & THEOLOGICAL STUDIES *by 1912 Faculty of Princeton*
THE POWER OF GOD UNTO SALVATION *by B.B. Warfield*
THE LORD OF GLORY *by B.B. Warfield*
A GENTLEMAN & A SCHOLAR: *Memoir of J.P. Boyce* *by J. Broadus*
SERMONS TO THE NATURAL MAN *by W.G.T. Shedd*
SERMONS TO THE SPIRITUAL MAN *by W.G.T. Shedd*
HOMILETICS AND PASTORAL THEOLOGY *by W.G.T. Shedd*
A PASTOR'S SKETCHES 1 & 2 *by Ichabod S. Spencer*
THE PREACHER AND HIS MODELS *by James Stalker*
IMAGO CHRISTI *by James Stalker*
A HISTORY OF PREACHING *by Edwin C. Dargan*
LECTURES ON THE HISTORY OF PREACHING *by J. A. Broadus*
THE SCOTTISH PULPIT *by William Taylor*
THE SHORTER CATECHISM ILLUSTRATED *by John Whitecross*
THE CHURCH MEMBER'S GUIDE *by John Angell James*
THE SUNDAY SCHOOL TEACHER'S GUIDE *by John A. James*
CHRIST IN SONG: *Hymns of Immanuel from All Ages* *by Philip Schaff*
COME YE APART: *Daily Words from the Four Gospels* *by J.R. Miller*
DEVOTIONAL LIFE OF THE S.S. TEACHER *by J.R. Miller*

www.ingramcontent.com/pod-product-compliance
Lightning Source LLC
Chambersburg PA
CBHW022109150426
43195CB00008B/325